Setting Up In Italy

Setting Up In Italy

Sebastian O'Kelly

MEREHURST
— LONDON —

To Kym and Andreas

without whose (different) encouragement
this would not have been possible ...

Published 1990 by Merehurst Limited
Ferry House, 51-57 Lacy Road,
Putney, London SW15 1PR.

© Sebastian O'Kelly 1990

ISBN 1 85391 084 X

Designed and produced by Snap! Books
Typeset by Broadview
Maps by Lovell Johns
Printed in Great Britain by Mackays of Chatham
plc, Chatham, Kent

Contents

Acknowledgements

This book owes much to the help provided by friends and people previously unknown to me who live permanently in Italy. Many of the latter patiently set aside many hours to explain the intricacies of Italian finance, conveyancing and local government, subjects which were not naturally their preferred topics of conversation. Above all I am grateful to Antonio Cardone. His hospitality in Rome and unceasing advice on virtually all matters, some of them connected with living in Italy, were of invaluable assistance. Mike Ivy, of the British Council in Naples, was enlightening about southern Italy, while Alex Kirichenko and Mark Walters, of International Consultancy Services, put me straight about business life in that singular city. Elisa Gazzi, of the Italian Institute, London, clarified the Italian education system. John Tunstill, Jim Powrie and David Newman, estate agents in Umbria, spent much time explaining local housing market conditions. Nicola Schmitt and Mark Mills did the same in Tuscany. Thanks too to Nikki Keep, of Italian Country Homes. Michael, Heather, Francesca and Benedict Goodhall, of San Gimignano, were hospitable and helpful. As was Francesca Davies, of the same town. Mike Bourgogne explained family law in Italy and Alan and Susan Wrightson, of Invitation to Tuscany, explained planning procedures. Charles Ross provided interesting information on the Emilia Romagna/Tuscany border, which is under-rated. George Pazzi-Axworthy, of Griffinhoofe, Lincoln's Inn, a solicitor also qualified in Italian law, was kind enough to read the manuscript. Thanks also to Jennifer Grego and John Wyles of the *Financial Times*'s Rome office. I envied Gordon McDougall his beautiful view.

Introduction

There is an advertisement on British television which goes something like this: an elderly, attractive lady is bent over the kitchen table and tears are running down her cheeks. A little boy watching her from the doorway, quickly turns and darts into the street. *Tonino, dove vai?* cries out a fruitseller, dressed in a waistcoat and cap. The boy does not stop, but runs on, sidestepping a couple of gesticulating old men in deep discussion in the middle of the cobbled street, and enters a shop. He buys something, handing his money to an avuncular shopkeeper. Back in the kitchen, the music - the intermezzo from *Cavalleria Rusticana* - rises to a sentimental crescendo. The little boy approaches the old lady and puts something on the table. It is a box of paper tissues. She stops chopping some onions, wipes her eyes and envelops the boy in her capacious bosom.

Such is life in Italy as interpreted by a West End advertising agency: picturesque mama, enchanting bambino and beaming townsfolk, who are the salt of the earth. As you move into your new home, say, on a Tuscan hilltop, the reality may well prove very different to this sugared ideal. Far from thinking about getting paper tissues for adults, the children may have already started whining about missing friends left behind in a place they will insist on calling "back home". The electricity may be cut off, or the water, or both, and the estate agent, who seemed so solicitous and charming, has not organised the removal of a pile of rubble from the front door as promised.

Hopefully, at more or less the same time you arrive at your new home so does your furniture. But when the driver of the pantechnicon eventually finds the right address, he shakes his head at the untarmaced country roads, and begins unloading your possessions then and there, three kilometres from the front door. It begins to drizzle, for, sad truth, it does indeed rain in Italy. At moments like these a neo-Georgian semi in Weybridge never seemed more attractive ...

Moving house is traumatic at the best of times. It is even more so when setting up home in another country. In Italy, local customs are perplexing and - a universal lament - the bureaucracy is a nightmare. While the neighbours are unfailingly friendly, they are also inquisitive. All have to be dealt with in stilted, evening class Italian, which frustratingly limits you to the conversational range of a six-year-old. Don't despair. Many others before you have been in the same position and survived. One of the pleasant discoveries in researching this book was that very few people who have made Italy their home have subsequently regretted the decision.

At the time of writing, many who talk of 1992 nod wisely and pronounce that its importance has been greatly exaggerated. The changes will not be great, nor speedy. Whether this proves to be the case or not, 1992 has had a seductive influence on the British. Never before has the grass on the other side of the Channel seemed greener, and now there seems little reason to stay off it. While their government has the reputation of being lukewarm towards Europe, the British themselves are among the most enthusiastic of all. For most Italians, the harmonization of Europe's frontiers is an economic event and, less importantly, a political one. But very few think that it is cause for setting up home outside Italy. Not so the British. It took a long time for the notion of a united Europe to catch on, but now that it has the British, or at any rate a good many of them, are eager to declare themselves what they always have been - European.

Recent years have seen an influx of British immigrants, who are now busy setting up home in the beautiful countryside of Tuscany and Umbria. There is no objective scale to balance the advantages and disadvantages of the move and conclude whether the quality of their lives has improved. Whether it has or whether it hasn't, for many people life is short and the fun is in giving it a go. The aim of this book is not to encourage readers to sell their homes in Britain and move out to Italy. That is a decision which must be made alone. But the aim is to provide practical advice and give a few warnings about the possible pitfalls. It also aims to introduce a complicated country, with wide regional differences, both in geography and, far more importantly, in culture. If there is any guiding principle about buying property in Italy which has been gleaned from talking to many British people who live there, it is simply this: there is no need to hurry. Take it all calmly, follow the rules and be prudent.

1 Setting the Scene

This book was written in the glorious summer of 1989, when one bright, sunny day routinely followed another and at times it was easy to forget that this was London and not Florence or Rome. In such conditions, it seemed strange to think that people would consider leaving the motherland to chance their luck at living elsewhere. Only when the weather chilled and the familiar glowering greyness returned, during November and December, did this brief period of contentment end. The "wingeing pom" in us all re-emerged. The summer, though wonderful, had been preceded by four pitiful apologies for the word. And autumn, the season of mellow fruitfulness, is always too sharp for comfort, while in Tuscany or Umbria it means, well, fruit. The grapes are being gathered and, long before mid-morning, the mists retreat before the warming sun. At home, with only December and January to look forward to, the appeal of "abroad" began to grow.

Of course, the weather is only an excuse, although a very plausible one. The truth is that the British, or at least an appreciable number of them, are only too happy to desert their home and hearth. Family, friends and everything that they know well are not enough to bind them. This disposition to travel and live in a foreign land may be intrepid or rather sad, depending on your point of view. It is, in any case, difficult for Italians to understand - their emotional attachment to home having long been a source of caricature. It also puzzled the author. While meeting British people now living in Putney-rustic farmhouses or black and white designer apartments in Rome, the question would always come up: why did you do it? Weather was not a satisfactory answer; it is the classic British evasion. Views and countryside account for a lot, but then the decidedly unpicturesque backstreets of Naples have their long-stay British residents. A few replies were patently insincere: "we wanted to be near the centres of European civilisation" or, more cunningly, "we did it for the children".

In the end an answer began to form. It is simple enough. The British think the Italians are more happy than they are. A tired-eyed salesman, met on a train to Sheffield, expressed this better than anyone I met in Italy. He had been to Amalfi several times on his holidays and his wife had worked in her teens as an *au pair* in Milan. They had often talked about living there. "The Italians have got it right," he said, drawing on a can of lager. "They understand that you work hard in order to improve the quality of your life; that there's no point to it unless that's your aim. What do we do? We get smashed on a Friday night."

Other north Europeans, suffering similiar sort of *angst* doubtless traceable to Protestantism, also make the move to Italy, where the sun is warmer and the religion more pagan. But so far as many of the Dutch and the Germans are concerned, who make up the other large foreign groupings in the villas and farmhouses of central Italy, they have left their home country because they did not happily fit in. As one Dutch lady, long resident in southern Tuscany and now pushing 45, explained with a touch of nostalgic defiance: "We are alternatives."

The same is not true of many of the British, who come to Italy in all varieties. There are pensioners who have bought small cottages in Umbria in preference to an apartment on the Spanish *costas* and there are young couples who want to bring up their children in sight of Lake Trasimeno rather than Tooting Common. Then again, in the business centres of Rome or Milan, there are the ex-pat high achievers, who ply their trade in financial services and expect, with 1992 and all that, to wipe the floor with the clod-hopping, state-controlled Italian banks.

David Newman, an estate agent based in Castiglione del Lago, in Umbria, reckons that about a third of his clients are in the media and allied trades, such as advertising or television, or they are lawyers, doctors and architects. Another third are what he calls "burned out yuppies", ex-City Big-Bangers who have come to Umbria to retreat from a competitive, hard world. The remaining third are older people, who have retired. Of these, many are long-term expatriates who have spent much of their working lives in places such as the Gulf or Hong Kong.

A surprising lack of records, and the recent rise in popularity of Umbria, makes estimates of the total number of British subjects living in Italy largely a matter of guesswork. The British Embassy in Rome thinks about 60,000 Britons own homes in Italy and between 30,000 and 40,000 live there permanently. The figure is in any case far lower than Spain, where there are 200,000 British homeowners. In France, there are about 44,000 permanent residents, with the same again owning holiday homes.

Outside Milan and Rome, the British "recreational" residents tend to live in fairly remote rural areas. There are, however, little British patches in the central Italian countryside. Chiantishire, between Florence and Siena, is the most well known. Its reputation is not totally deserved, however. The foreigners who live in the area, with the town of Greve at its centre, are of all nationalities. You are as likely to bump into Germans as British in the surrounding bars and restaurants. But Chianti is expensive, and this has created a certain envy among those who live in the less fashionable areas. It is said that the well-heeled who live there have successfully introduced cherished snobberies and social distinctions, which would be more at home in Surrey. Shameless scenes are alleged to take place as members of the British community grovel for dinner party invitations from the local nobility and wine-producers.

There may be some truth in this, or it could all be sour grapes. Those who most eagerly relate these tales usually have a wide streak of snobbery themselves, but of the inverse variety. In certain British sets in Umbria, where teachers and middle-ranking media functionaries have converted farm cottages, sound, right-on values are essential. Here women moan about the "sexism" of Italian men and everyone thanks their lucky stars that they have escaped "Thatcher's Britain". They adopt almost the posture of refugees and ungratefully forget the property boom and ending of exchange controls, which allowed them to flee to Italy in the first place.

Where clusters of British residents have developed it is because they have all gone to the same estate agent, of which there are very few in Italy. So it is that around Città di Castello and Umbertide, in Umbria, there are quite high concentrations of British people. However, in nearby Le Marche, which has a similar countryside and Urbino as well, not many Britons, or foreigners of any type, have set up home. The same is true of northern Lazio and southern Emilia Romagna.

Outside Chianti and the area around Lucca, which is also expensive, the British living in Tuscany are quite well spread out. If you do not want to come across fellow countrymen there is plenty of space to ensure that you need not do so. It is also the case that the British in Tuscany have tended to live there for far longer than those in Umbria, who have in the main arrived in the last four years. As a result, their relations with the locals are often very close. Their children have gone to local schools, made friends and have acquired Italian values. Smaller children, who have started primary school, often talk to their parents in a strange mismatch of Italian and English. For all the young families who move permanently to Italy, education is a principal concern. Italian schools, discussed later, have their shortcomings. But as one ex-Londoner living in Naples, referring to his son, said: "I would rather he became a *scugnizzo* (urchin) than a skinhead."

From the above, it must be clear that it is going to be difficult to re-create a corner of Britain in the Italian countryside. In central Italy, the British communities are small and are likely to play only a part in your life. Elsewhere, in the South for example, you are quite likely never to meet a fellow countryman unless you make a special effort. There is no comparison with life on the *costas*, where vast international communities have sprung up and many foreigners never bother to learn Spanish. Fortunately, in no part of Italy is this possible. In some form or another, the language must be mastered. The Italian bureaucracy, if nothing else, will see to that. State institutions have an aversion to letters or correspondence of any kind. Matters have to be dealt with face-to-face. For those who are busy and have better things to do, hours of frustration are wasted wrangling at the town hall. Others have warmed to this way of doing things. One pensioner who now lives alone finds her battles with the local comune an enjoyable interlude in what can be a lonely life.

Nor is it possible once living in Italy to retreat from it for very long, however many hectares you own or fences you put up. Italians everywhere are an intensely curious people. Those who live there, particularly in out of the way areas, must expect local people to drop in for a chat or to discuss at great length a minor problem, which has a solution obvious to all. The idea that these visits may not be welcome does not cross their minds. In many cases, non-Italian speaking families are virtually adopted by the locals who provide invaluable assistance coping with the local regulations and the comune. Italy is a country where you need friends in order to get on.

It is rare to hear of people who moved to Italy and found they disliked it. In most cases where this has happened it has involved pensioners, who knew little of the country beforehand. One couple bought property in a seaside town in Campania, expecting to find there the year-round social life that exists on the *costas*. The culture of the villagers was very different to what they were familiar with and evening class Italian was not enough to master the local dialect. In summer the resort was over-run by Neapolitans and English-speaking foreigners were rare. Few places are more dismal than these resorts in winter and the couple eventually decided to leave.

The biggest disappointments are felt by those who think that Italy will be cheap. It isn't. Apart from rural housing, which the Italians are not - yet - interested in, it is difficult to think of many things which are less expensive than in Britain. Cheap booze and tobacco were the traditional continental enticements, but they are not enough to live on. When Italians come to Britain they are amazed by the low prices. High quality clothes cost far less in London department stores than they do in Rome or Milan - even when they are made in Italy. Most food is cheaper in England, although Italians are deeply suspicious about the quality. British furniture, silverware, cutlery, antique prints and paintings seem incredibly good value. There is a booming antique export business to Italy, as newly wealthy Italians seek to hint at older money in their designer decorated apartments. In exchange, Milan sells in Britain inferior matt black designer knick-knacks, rather in the way that eighteenth-century traders short-changed primitives with coloured beads.

Charles, formerly a theatre director in Britain, moved to Umbria with his wife and two daughters last year. His job had taken him all over the world and for long periods he would have to live on university campuses in the American Midwest. The novelty had worn off and he wanted to spend more time with his family. They thought about buying a place in Wales or Scotland, but in the end settled for Umbria. Charles had spent a lot of time in Italy in the 1960s and assumed that the comparative price differences of those days still prevailed. "We thought it would not cost much to live in Italy once we had bought the house. I had hoped to spend about £5,000 a year until renting off half the villa began to bring in cash. We learned very quickly we were being absurd."

The wealthy are cushioned against the high cost of living in Italy. Suzanne's motives for moving to Italy are interesting and worth mentioning in detail. But money was never a difficulty. Until two years ago Suzanne, who is 42, and has two daughters, lived in a large house on Richmond Hill, in south-west London. Her husband is the director of a publicly quoted British company. They were well off, but Suzanne was bored with the life she was leading.

"Richmond had become very routine. You have a nice big house and a nice big car. Then your husband gets a pay rise and you get an even bigger house and an even bigger car. You start having even bigger dinner parties for a whole lot of people you do not really know. And then things get competitive. There is no point at all in living that kind of life unless you get to the top of it. I just got fed up. I did not like Richmond particularly, always meeting the same people as I dropped my daughter off to school, going to children's parties and so on. As the daughter of a soldier, I was used to travelling about and I have lived in Singapore, Beirut and east Africa. So we thought about and decided to buy a place here."

"Here" is a delightful, modernised farmhouse in central Tuscany, which has 35 hectares given over to vines producing Vernaccia. This is now the family home, where Suzanne lives with her daughters, mother and two rottweilers. The house in Richmond has been sold and her husband, now living in a bachelor flat in London, flies over to Pisa every four weeks or so for a long weekend. It is an arrangement that has worked very happily.

Since making the move, Suzanne's life has been enriched in other ways. She explained: "I had become stuck in a rut. I had been married for 10 years to a man who is really quite forceful and dominating. Before I had married, I had run my own business and I was used to taking charge of my own life. Gradually, I felt I was losing this part of my character. But out here I am in charge of everything. If the tractor goes wrong, I have to get it fixed. If the lights go out, which they do frequently, I must make sure all the torches work. I have to deal with the comune, for residence permits, for water and to get the children to school. The bureaucracy here is a killer. But it has all been worth it. It is good fun."

In spite of spending most days putting the farm in order, Suzanne has made friends with British people who live locally and her six-year-old daughter, who goes to the local school, speaks fluent Italian. Mother and the rottweilers have had the most difficulty settling in: mother because she missed friends in England and will not learn the language; the rottweilers because they occasionally take on local porcupine, with painful consequences. There are no regrets about making the move and Suzanne feels the quality of her life has improved immensely.

With a touch of Richmond Hill returning to her conversation, Suzanne says that she gets on well with other English people, but that the younger ones often "have something dodgy about them, as though they have failed at home". This is a harsh judgement. There is some truth in the view that Italy attracts a disproportionate amount of vaguely professional people in their 30s with no visible means of support. But in time they prosper and even in rural Italy businesses flourish. Estate agents and those in the villa renting business make high earnings by any standard. One boasts of an income in excess of £35,000 and, like many Italians, he pays no income tax at all. Others have opened riding establishments, set up as electricians or computer consultants, give English lessons or do technical translations.

The ambitions of many who have made the move to Italy are somewhat ambiguous. Although they have played truant to normal careers in Britain, they retain quite conventional hopes for their children. Annie, now in her mid-30s, was a rock and roll journalist who exchanged a flat in Clapham for a farm worker's cottage near Lake Trasimeno. One reason for making the move was to bring up her young son, aged four, in a more attractive environment than south London. It was not simply a question of the open fields and trees of Umbria. Most of all she wanted him to grow up experiencing the traditional values which over the years Annie herself had so heartily rejected.

She explained: "Your attitude changes when you have children. I did not want to bring up my son where there is violence and, worse of all, drugs. You just start getting very protective. I know these are awful double standards and I am a complete hypocrite, but Italy just seemed a better bet. On the other hand I do not want my son to become completely part of the community here. I don't want him to be going steady with a girl when he is 14, engaged by 17 or so and married by 20. I do not want him to be drawn into the kind of life where the most he would be able to do would be to work in the local comune. I just hope that because we frequently go back to England and have friends and family there, he will have a broader horizon and want more out of life."

Many of the younger people who move permanently to these areas of Italy are what the Dutch woman above referred to as "alternatives", people who in an earlier age would have been described as bohemian. The majority are university educated and many have worked in the arts: dancers, actresses, media types, architects, designers and so forth. An appreciable number are homosexuals. The notion of the loving, monogamous gay couple is alien to Italy, as it is in most of the world. But although the locals might find these attachments strange, they are essentially tolerant. Violence against gays, along with other non-profitable forms of thuggery, have not taken root. Nor has there been any attempt at state repression. Unlike Britain, homosexuality has never been illegal in Italy. The idea that the government should in some way improve the morals of the nation would probably strike most Italians as laughable. Of, course, the church does not approve, and never has. In the Middle Ages, it would occasionally burn sodomites, giving rise to the curious word for a homosexual in central and northern Italy: *un finocchio*, a fennel. Apparently fennel would be thrown on to the pyre to mask the smell of burning flesh.

Although locals are puzzled by the new arrivals to the countryside there is very little resentment towards them. Richer Florentines are supposed to be annoyed that they missed the boat in buying into Chianti, and now find the area too expensive. But on the whole the foreigners are welcome and the British well thought of. The traditional view of the distinguished Englishman abroad still has weight with the locals. But more up-to-date impressions of the British are creeping through. A Tuscan farm worker told me in all seriousness that the British were more prone to molest children than other nationalities (he had heard something of the Cleveland affair on Italian television). This unsavoury aspect of the British national character was on top of other better known defects: drunkenness and hooliganism. Memories of the Heysel Stadium slaughter remain strong in Italy.

One reason for the warm reception of strangers to the central Italian countryside may be the fact that the area is well used to accommodating aliens. Since the war, Italy has undergone an incredible rate of urbanisation with the result that the countryside has become depopulated. In the Sixties, Sardinians were encouraged with give-away loans to move to newly vacated hill farms in Tuscany and Umbria. Now even this flow has stopped. Only 22 per cent of Italians live in villages or isolated homes, the rest are in towns. Consequently the arrival of the foreigners has revived the local economy. Building firms, agricultural contract firms and village shopkeepers have all benefited. So too have local farmers, now able to sell ruinous old houses for sums of money that would have been unimaginable even a few years ago. There is a cost involved in this, however, and it is not purely economic. Foreigners who have bought hill farms, turning old ploughs and threshing machines into flower stands and other rustic adornments, have been visited occasionally by emotional locals who well remember working on the farm that had been in their family for generations. Many regret parting with their old homes for such comparatively small sums of money.

There are also those who are convinced that the Italians themselves are soon to take a revived interest in their countryside. The government is giving generous subsidies for what is called *agriturismo*. This term encompasses hiking, riding, bird spotting and similar country activities. Farmers can now offer bed and breakfast accommodation, which is regarded as an agricultural activity so far as subsidies and taxes are concerned. Most Italians take their holidays in Italy, and in summer that means the coast. But these days the seaside is not as appealing as it once was. There is massive overcrowding, particularly in August. Much of what was once delightful coastline has been spoilt by the worse kind of merit-free architectural sprawl. And, most serious of all, the Italians are waking up to the fact that the sea itself is often disgustingly dirty. The algal bloom which killed off the tourist season in the Adriatic in 1989 has finally brought this home. One consequence could well be a surge in demand for *agriturismo* holidays. Rural house prices in attractive areas could shoot up and the Italians will move back in. To an extent this has already happened in southern Umbria, around Orvieto, where rich Italians have stylish country villas. An Umbrian, with typical provincial chauvinism, said that the majority of foreigners - *stranieri* - in Umbria were Romans.

This is an important development for those who are considering buying a rural retreat as an investment. It is difficult to get any figures on price movements because at the moment foreigners are setting the pace of the market and the prices are whatever they are prepared to pay. According to John Tunstill, an estate agent in Umbria who sells property (much of it his own), prices have gone up by 30 per cent a year. Since 1984, when he began, Tunstill has sold 121 houses and the average prices were as follows:

1984-85	£15,000
1985-86	£18,000
1986-87	£20,000
1987-88	£26,000
1988-89	£31,000

These prices are for houses which will require considerable expense to be modernised and this is discussed later.

The investment seems attractive and Tunstill is convinced prices will rise still further. As he puts it: "Umbria is like the Cotswolds 20 years ago." However, all estate agents in Italy in summer 1989 reported a marked fall in interest from British buyers. The reason for this is undoubtedly the slump in British property prices. A contributing factor is the state of the economy, experiencing what, at time of writing, the British government refers to as "a soft landing". Interest from the Swiss, Dutch and Germans was as strong as ever. Understandably, given their own beautiful countryside, the French are not interested at all.

THE ESSENTIAL CHECK-LIST

There are bound to be many personal factors which will determine your decision whether or not to buy a property in Italy. Before embarking on what is going to be a massive upheaval in your life and involve great expense, it might be wise to consider some general questions concerning your various needs and the practicality of the choices before you:

Your motives

The first question that must be resolved is whether the house you are buying is to be your permanent home or a holiday retreat. If you intend to live out your days in Italy you must have a clear idea of why you are doing it and what you expect to gain. For most people the decision to move to a foreign country involves a complete change in their day-to-day life.

Those who want to buy a holiday home should ask themselves whether they are actually going to use it. Many who own property in Italy seldom live there, which is why there are so many villa rental agencies. You may feel obliged to spend time at your new home, even though you would prefer taking your holidays elsewhere. Remember, too, that owning any property involves spending a certain amount of time looking after it. Flats and homes in service-run complexes are much less of a problem than country houses. Finding someone to look after things when you are away can be difficult, sometimes impossible. Be prepared to deal - at a distance - with exactly the same kind of difficulties you would experience in Britain: burst pipes, leaking roofs, no electricity etc.

People who move to Italy for work reasons are likely to have most choices concerning where and how they live already decided for them. It is difficult to live in a pleasant rural house and commute into Milan everyday. Most Italians live in cities, in flats with less space and fewer household possessions than the British. You must decide whether this lifestyle is what you want.

Collecting your pension and heading off into the sun is an attractive notion, but you have also got to make sure that it is a practical one. Rather than living permanently in Italy, away from family, familiar neighbours and friends, it may be better to have simply a small second home there. Give the matter of what you would do in Italy, day by day, a degree of thought.

Your choices

Consider the implications of your decision on where to live. Some houses in the country have breathtaking scenery. But will this be enough? Such a life can be cut-off and unless you have lots of resources of your own it can be very boring. Those who want to enter into Italian life would be more at home in or near small villages or towns. While it may not be your principal intention to live in Italy close to fellow expatriates, they will have overcome exactly the same initial problems which are facing you. Their advice can be invaluable. Certain parts of rural Italy are rather sleepy, and it could well be that the other foreigners provide the only social life going.

Coastal resorts, perhaps fortunately, lack the international presence on the Spanish *costas*. The crowds are there, but they are Italians. Any property within sight of the sea is expensive in Italy, although obviously cheaper in the far south, away from the *autostrade*. Very little of the coastline is pleasantly secluded. If sea and sand are your main motives for moving to Italy, you will have to choose your retreat with care.

The division between North and South is crucial in Italy, and there is a markedly different outlook on life. The South is more poor, more lackadaisical, and Mediterranean. Even Rome is a sleepy city compared with the commercial push and shove of Milan. But the South is considered friendlier. These differences should influence your decision on where to live.

Considerations

There are many other questions to answer before you decide to move to Italy. Can you afford it? What kind of work could you do? Do you need commercial facilities and good communications? Does it matter if the region you have fallen in love with has poor communications and no airport? Do you need a car? Are the locally prevailing standards of education or health care important? Will you need sport and leisure facilities (remember these are seldom available in Italian schools)? Do you need access to good shops?

2 The Regions of Italy

In spite of its reputation Italy is not, geographically, a very hospitable land. Cut off from the rest of Europe by the natural frontier of the Alps, most of the peninsula is mountain or hills. Only 23 per cent of the land is agriculturally rich plain. Indeed, 35 per cent of the land surface is above 2,300 feet. In comparison, the British Isles are accommodating lumps of mud. It has been Italy's particular misfortune that once over the Alps its largest and most fertile plain begins almost immediately. The triangle of the Po valley, from Turin to Venice and down to Ravenna, is virtually without hills or natural defences of any kind. Along with the Low Countries, this area of northern Italy has been the battlefield of Europe. Few major wars have not involved it in some way, as the defensive architecture from all ages testifies. When the barbarian menace threatened the Roman empire, its strategic importance was well appreciated. The defence against the invaders was organised from Milan, which grew from a barracks town to rival the size of Rome itself. When Milan fell, so did Rome, although what remained of civilisation did continue at Ravenna, safe for a time behind impenetrable swamps.

Below Bologna begin the Appenines, and the straight, grid-like roads of Emilia Romagna give way to the indeterminate squiggles of Tuscany, where traffic has always had to follow the contours of the land. For all the beauty of its gentle, manicured hills, Tuscan agriculture, outside the cultivation of vines, is small-scale, low profit and in crisis. Only in the south of the region, in the Maremma, is the land flat and rich in a plain which continues into Lazio, north of Rome.

South of the capital are fertile hills and the rich Pontine marshes, successfully drained by Mussolini. Thereafter begins the Mezzogiorno, literally the Mid-day, as the South is known. The Appenines, which are mainly habitable in central Italy, transform into the higher and far harsher Abruzzi. Wooded hill tops are replaced by bald rock. There are rich agricultural areas, for example, the slopes of Vesuvius, which accounted for Pompei's wealth, and the Gulf of Salerno. But they are small and remote. This agricultural poverty has been a principal reason why the provinces in the South could not sustain the kind of independent states which made up most of northern Italy. From the middle ages until the last century the South has always been a political whole, known as the Kingdom, *il regno*, to distinguish it from the lesser principalities in the peninsula. The one rich agricultural area in an otherwise picturesque but poor land, is the Tavoliere in Puglia. Since 1945, this vast plain has been successfully irrigated by distant waters and it is now the main producing area in Italy of olive oil, grapes and citrus fruits.

There are pronounced differences in climate between the regions. The following table indicates average monthly temperatures (centigrade) and rainfall (millimetres) in key centres.

	January		April		July		October	
Main cities	Temp	Rain	Temp	Rain	Temp	Rain	Temp	Rain
Cagliari	9.9°	54	15.3°	43	25.8°	3	19.5°	53
Florence	5.6°	61	13.3°	74	25°	23	15.8°	96
Genoa	8.4°	109	14.5°	82	24.6°	35	18.1°	135
Milan	1.9°	62	13.2°	82	24.8°	47	13.7°	75
Naples	8.7°	87	14.3°	55	24.8°	14	18.1°	102
Palermo	10.3°	141	16.2°	65	25.3°	6	19.9°	123
Rome	7.4°	74	14.4°	62	25.7°	6	17.7°	123
Turin	0.3°	11	12°	74	23.2°	65	12.2°	59
Venice	3.8°	58	12.6°	77	23.6°	37	15.1°	66

Generally speaking, the South is Mediterranean, while the North, apart from its coastline, does not feel Mediterranean at all. The centre is a mixture of the two. In winter, the Alps are cold but dry, while the Italian Riviera is mild. The Po valley tends to be very wet and cold, as is Venice, and the Adriatic generally. Central Italy is quite mild in low lying areas, but the hills are cold and occasionally there is snow. The *autostrade* can be snow-bound. The Abruzzi are very barren and freezing in winter. The South and Sicily are mild. Even in December the days can be sunny and quite warm, although it cools down markedly at night. In summer, many find the South too hot and parched. The grass in Tuscany and Umbria is seldom completely frazzled.

The geographic isolation of one province from another, and their often widely varying historical development, has allowed strong regional differences to persist in Italy. Not only do manners and mores vary, but so too does language. Most Italians can easily speak some kind of dialect with their neighbour which would be incomprehensible to Italians from elsewhere, let alone foreigners. Great pride is taken in this. If you ask an Italian citizen what is his country - *paese* - he is far more likely to say with pride "Naples", "Turin" or "Pisa" than, more prosaically, "Italy". A wonderful Italian word sums up this provincial chauvinism which extends even to villages: *campanilismo*, from *campanile*, a church bell tower. One of the worst offenders is probably Siena. Not only do its citizens loathe the Florentines, who conquered them in the sixteenth century, they dislike even those who live in different parishes of the city, the *contrade*. These loyalties come to the fore during the *palio* horse race. It all seems rather strange in a city whose great days came to an end with the Black Death of 1348.

While the usually good humoured rivalry of *campanilismo* is an interesting dimension of Italian culture, the dislike between southerners and northerners is now becoming quite serious. In the summer of 1989, an Air Force officer, who was a southerner, was set upon by thugs in Verona and stabbed to death after they heard him say goodnight to a friend with a southern accent. There are the beginnings of a serious social problem here and the Italian press rightly describes it as *razzismo*, racism. In the 1989 European elections the Lombard League won two seats in Strasbourg on a platform opposed to southern immigration to the North. The League wants to limit jobs, particularly teaching posts, to northerners and fulminates against alien southern values, such as the *mafia's* code of honour, which are corrupting the honest *bon bourgeois* North. But the League denies that it is racist, claiming it has nothing against black immigrants, only southern Italians. As well as seats in Strasbourg the League has a senator and a deputy in parliament. All the other regions of the North have smaller autonomy parties which have helped to whip up passions against the despised southern *terroni*, or bumpkins. These days when families make their way up to the North to watch the Naples football team, thuggish elements, of which there are quite a few particularly in Verona, shout "Take a wash" and, more insultingly, "Cholera! Cholera!", a reference to the epidemic in Naples in the early 1970s.

Dislike between northerners and southerners has been a perennial feature of Italy ever since the state was unified. The South has always thought, with some justification, that it has been treated as a conquered land and its comparative wealth has declined. The North, on the other hand, feels it expends vast sums on economic aid which is greedily trousered by the South's ubiquitous criminal elements. There is truth in this too. While southerners are insulted as *terroni*, northerners are called *polentoni*, eaters of *polenta*, the maize flower stodge popular in the North. The new bitterness in this age-old rivalry is a consequence of Italy's success, its *sorpasso*. Southerners coming to the North for work are no longer the impoverished immigrants who 40 years ago used to arrive at Milan station clutching a cardboard suitcase ready to take any wages offered. These days they are being appointed to high posts within the public administration, after winning *concorsi*, the state examinations. Throughout the North, high-ranking police officers, health service doctors, magistrates, judges and teachers are southerners. The northern middle class has long since deserted these important but relatively low paying jobs for more attractive careers in the private sector. But the northern lower middle and working classes take exception to being taught, or told what to do, or fined by Sicilians, Calabrians and Neapolitans. Nothing much is going to be done about this problem, or indeed can be done. Doubtless, the Italian parliament will pass a resounding declaration underlining the importance of preserving unique regional cultures. In the nineteenth century the Austrian Prince Metternich brushed aside demands for an Italian nation by describing Italy as merely a geographical expression. The development of these regional autonomy parties, which look back to the fragmented states of pre-unification Italy with nostalgia, demonstrate that there is a strong element of truth in that statement even today.

There are 20 regions in Italy and these are divided into 95 provinces, the initials of which are to be found on car number plates.

Regions of Italy

The following pages aim to give a brief introduction to the various regions of Italy, summarising the main geographical features and the type of society one can expect to find.

TUSCANY

It appears to be difficult to describe Tuscany in less than hyperbolic terms. Pick up any travel book and similar phrases will be found: Tuscany is the "heart of Italy", the "cradle of art", the "birthplace of the Renaissance". All are true enough. Situated in the centre of the country, the region possesses the best of both North and South. Its climate is neither northern Italian nor is it completely Mediterranean. On its gentle hills are cypresses and olive groves, the furthest north you will find them except along the western coastline. Yet there are also woods of deciduous trees which give the countryside, particularly in autumn, beautiful colours. Low lying hills vary the landscape, making it intimate and welcoming. Small villages nestle in the valleys. For anyone travelling down from the North, it is a delightful contrast with the damp and dull plains of Emilia Romagna. Unlike Lazio, to the south, where the landscape again widens becoming more harsh and barren, the summer in Tuscany is seldom so hot that the land loses its green.

For all the beauty of the countryside, it is the cities of Tuscany, and the art they contain, which draw visitors from all over the world. Florence, and everything that it represents, is one of the finest achievements of the West. It may no longer be in the front rank of cities, but few Italians would not concede that it is the true centre of their culture: Rome was too occupied with the Church; Milan, dominated by despots, was French-leaning and favoured gothic art; and Venice always looked first to the Orient. Florence, through cloth-making and banking, grew into the finest city of all and was also the most Italian. Even the language evolved from Tuscan dialect.

Tuscany has for centuries attracted a disproportionate share of British visitors. One of the earliest was Sir John Hawkwood, a ruthless mercenary captain, who found employment in Tuscany after a lull in the Hundred Years War resulted in his sudden redundancy. Florence, strangely grateful given Hawkwood's treacherous nature, even buried him in the cathedral. Conan Doyle's novel *The White Company* concerns his adventures. Others to have set up home in the city have included Robert and Elisabeth (Barrett) Browning, who after their secret marriage in 1849 lived in the Piazza San Felice, where their home can still be visited. Most grand tourists spent prolonged stays in the city. Florence Nightingale owes her name to having been born there (her elder sister, born in Naples, was called Parthenope). More recently, the Sitwells held court in their villa outside the city and, today, Sir Harold Acton, the historian, is the doyen of the British residents.

At no time in the past has Tuscany been more popular with the British than today. There are about 8,000 of them living permanently in the region, and a good many more own holiday homes. It must be said that for all the attractions of Florence or Siena, they are difficult places to live in. Apart from during the winter months, the cities are packed with tourists. The excessive numbers are a serious strain on local amenities and patience, and can rob even the most beautiful piazza of its charm. Like Venice, the comune of Florence talks of restricting numbers, arguing for better quality tourists rather than mass. But, of course, there is no solution that would not involve unacceptable restrictions. It is a feature of tourism, particularly the deadeningly unimaginative coach parties, only to visit a limited number of the most important sites. So even in Florence in summer there are parts of the city which remain enjoyable. Most foreigners who live there permanently, however, either work or study in the city.

The vast majority of foreigners who have settled Tuscany over the past 15 years live in the countryside, often in delightful old farmhouses. The most popular area is between Florence and Siena, the notorious "Chiantishire", although Lucca, too, has a high proportion of foreign residents. Elsewhere, the British in Tuscany are fairly well spread about, so there is little difficulty in avoiding them altogether if that is your intention. It is worth noting that Tuscany is a big place, being 22,991 sq km in area with a population of 3.5 million. The region is divided into nine provinces: Arezzo, Firenze, Grosseto, Livorno, Lucca, Massa Carrara, Pisa, Pistoia and Siena.

Many would consider that the most desirable address to have would be in Chiantishire. Although condemned for supposedly being snobbish, Chianti is a pleasant area to live in. Surprisingly, it does not feel typically Tuscan. The hills are covered, of course, with endless acres of vines and the summits are topped with large areas of deciduous woodland. But the landscape is large and from high points there are wide panoramas. It seems to lack the small scale and intimacy of other parts of Tuscany, such as around Colle di Val d'Elsa or in the lower-lying areas around San Gimignano. For all that, it is beautiful.

Chianti is well served with communications. Both Florence and Siena are nearby and the international airport at Pisa, often a crucial consideration for those living in Tuscany, is about one and a half to two hours away. To the east, is the Milan to Rome A1 *autostrade del sole,* and to the west is the dual carriageway (*superstrada*) between Florence and Siena. Express trains, including international trains, and the even faster *rapido* pass through Florence. Siena's rail links are not so good, but there are the slower *diretto* trains. Coaches can take you to Rome faster. In Chianti, apart from Greve, the main shopping centre is the Poggibonsi, a small town of limited picturesque appeal, but apparently good shops. If Poggibonsi's schools and health care do not fulfil your needs, the proximity of Florence, where there are several private schools and hospitals, may be a great advantage. The wine, which in straw covered flagons adorned gingham table-tops in swinging Sixties *trattorie,* is not considered to be up to much compared with the great wines of the world or, indeed, with other wines in Tuscany. Even Chianti Classico, with the coveted black cockerel label, is not highly rated.

It is difficult to be precise about the price of housing in Chianti. It is higher than most of Tuscany, but there are often variations in the general state of the property on offer. Even in Chianti, the occasional ruin comes onto the market. For example, a *casa colonica* (regional farmhouse) needing complete structural repairs, with eight rooms on the first floor, and animal stalls below (see Renovations, p.116) and eight hectares of olive groves, all within three kilometres from Greve cost £82,500 in 1989. A comparison can be made with a fully restored *casa colonica* outside Castagnoli, near Gaiole in Chianti. Built in the eighteenth century, on the ground floor the main building has an original bread oven, two outbuildings, kitchen, porticoes, large stables and cellar. On the first floor are three bedrooms, a sitting room and a bathroom. Another room has been built in the dovecot. The whole building is arranged around a courtyard. Outside are a large garden, olive and almond trees, a shrine to Our Lady and a 10 x 5 metres swimming pool. Asking price: £239,580.

Most of the property around Chianti is of this latter type, with a fair number of larger mansions and converted manor houses. Prices for flats or small villas in managed complexes are disproportionately higher than ordinary houses. With the slump in property in Britain, many property companies are now buying up old convents, estates and even deserted villas in central Italy. Nowhere more so than in Tuscany.

The area around Lucca shares with Chianti a certain exclusivity. The city itself is incredibly beautiful and the roads are very convenient. Pisa airport is about an hour away and the A11 *autostrade* to Florence and (A12) Genoa are nearby. There are regular bus services to Florence, Prato, Pistoia and Pisa. There is a station, but the railway is not a primary line. Prices of houses - converted *case calonniche*, modern sea view villas and grand country retreats - are quite high, although they fall sharply in the more mountainous areas north of the city along the Serchio valley towards Castelnuovo di Garfagnana. Here, between the Apuan Alps and the Appenines, the geography more resembles high Liguria than Tuscany. The province is named after the joined towns of Massa and Carrara (Carrara is where Michelangelo, and many others, obtained their marble). In winter there are frosts and Florentines go skiing at Abetone. In the nineteenth century, Bagni di Lucca was very popular. It had the first casino in Europe and there is even a Protestant cemetery. Barga has quite a large British population. In general, however, the remote tip of north western Tuscany attracts fewer foreign residents than around Lucca, which is where the main hospitals, schools and shops are to be found.

Many people apparently buy property in places such as Camaiore because of the sea views. This seems strange. The north west coast of Tuscany is not in the least attractive. A vast beach extends from La Spezia to Livorno and is given over to the worst type of seaside over-development. For centuries it was a neglected area, a strip of sand and then pine forests and malarial swamp. Little happened in these parts, although Shelley was washed up at Viareggio after putting to sea in a storm. His house still stands in Lerici, across the border in Liguria. The sea itself is filthy dirty and the beaches are packed out. Apart from visiting Pisa, where there is a fine university, there is little reason to spend much time on the northern Tuscan coast. The main Genoa to Rome railway travels down the coast, with some trains from Paris and Switzerland.

An area quite popular with foreigners is Le Crete, south of Siena. *Creta* means clay in Italian, and the landscape here is made up of undulating hills of corn fields. It was a rich agricultural area, but too small to compete with the prairies of Lombardy or Emilia Romagna. As with many other rural areas of central Italy, Le Crete has suffered from depopulation as locals have left the land for more lucrative employment. The little village of Lucignano d'Asso, for example, had a population of 300 people 30 years ago. Today only 20 remain. The depopulation, as well as the landscape itself, emit a faintly eerie feeling. The corn fields come right up to the solitary farmhouses, which are usually quite large. Many are exposed on the top of a knoll and do not give the impression of being very private. Some people love Le Crete, others find it a little forbidding and "lunar". There are pleasant little valleys between the hills which have streams and woods and here those who prefer more intimate surroundings have made their homes. The small towns in the area, Buonconvento, Asciano, are very pleasant. Pienza is a masterpiece of Renaissance architecture. The nearest centre is Siena.

Locals in Le Crete are as likely to be Sardinians as Tuscans. A Frenchman, one of very few living in Tuscany, pulled back the curtains one morning to see machine-gun wielding *Carabinieri* striding over the corn fields. They had decided to swoop on the local Sards in a round-up of drug dealers, thieves and other petty criminals. Even the family who drove around in a Ferrari had their house searched, simply because they were Sards. There is little love lost between the Tuscans and these rural immigrants. To the south of Le Crete are produced what are considered by many to be Tuscany's finest wines, Montepulciano and, best of all, the Brunello di Montalcino.

To get to Pisa or Florence from Le Crete would take a couple of hours. Rome, on the motorway, would only be a little more. The distance from Florence, more than anything else, probably accounts for the lower prices. In 1989 an old farmhouse with a hectare of land, near the medieval village of Montisi, was offered for sale at £51,000. It needed total reworking, but there were five rooms on the first floor and a similar amount of space in the animal stalls below. It had also had a "360° panorama", in other words it stands in splendid isolation on a knoll like many farmhouses in Le Crete.

San Gimignano, which is north west of Siena, is more expensive and probably more popular. Again it is closer to Florence and Pisa. In the countryside around the town, there is a richer agriculture than either Chianti or Le Crete. Crops of all kinds are grown in low lying and well watered fields. Whereas in Le Crete winters may be bleak, especially in a house enjoying a 360° panorama, the summers in breezeless valleys around San Gimignano may be too warm for many. San Gimignano is a beautiful, but unrelaxing small town. It is completely given over to the tourist trade (unlike Pienza in Le Crete) and the locals have seen rather too many foreigners in their time. The local wine is the white Vernaccia, the "vernage" of Chaucer.

A farmhouse of similar size and condition to the one described above at Montisi was recently advertised for £109,000. It is situated 15 minutes from San Gimignano, it had about a hectare of land, including cypresses and olives, and some outbuildings. The house was described as "basically sound, but needs refurbishing". Again, Poggibonsi is the nearest small town to San Gimignano and more serious business would have to be dealt with in Siena, about 40 minutes drive away. To get to Pisa airport would take over an hour. There are buses, but no trains.

An area to date rather neglected by estate agents is the area south of Volterra and Colle di Val d'Elsa. Stretching into the Colline Metallifere, this part of Tuscany is without main roads or rail links. But it is quite close to Siena to the east and about an hour or so from Pisa. It is pleasantly rural with little of fashionable Chiantishire about it. Volterra itself is a fascinating town, surrounded by ancient Etruscan walls. It is very high and exposed, and few foreigners actually live there. D.H. Lawrence was among many who moaned about its freezing climate, even in summer. Beautiful and not badly priced alabaster, which is the town's main industry, may be worth investigating for home furnishing. Property prices are on a par with Le Crete, although the chances of coming up with a bargain are probably greater.

Apart from being one of the most beautiful cities in Tuscany, Arezzo is surrounded by lovely countryside. The hills begin to get slightly steeper and more wooded. This trend becomes more pronounced in Umbria, not far to the east. Arezzo is equidistant from Florence and Perugia and well placed for the A1 *autostrada*. It is also situated on a main railway line. With the motorways, getting to Pisa does not take as long as the distance might suggest.

Prices around Arezzo, and Pieve San Stefano and San Sepolcro, to the east, and Cortona, to the south, are less than in western Tuscany. Typically unrestored large *case calonniche* would cost around £30,000 to £40,000 in 1989. An old stone farmhouse (dated stone, 1799) near Sansepolcro, with eight rooms on three floors was recently on sale for £19,900. An extremely old terraced house in the *centro storico* of the town (which was the birth place of Piero della Francesca and has his Resurrection in the local museum) was on offer for £15,500.

The two areas of Tuscany least affected by the influx of foreigners are the industrial sprawl around Pistoia and Prato and the south west, the Maremma, in the province of Grossetto. The reason for the lack of popularity of the former is pretty obvious, although there are pleasant places to live in the valleys towards Emilia Romagna, which are not far from Florence. The Maremma is an isolated, rural part of Tuscany. It is not suitable for anyone needing fast communications, indeed Rome is not much further away than Florence, and quicker to get to with a *superstrada* from Grossetto running along the coast and linking up with the A12 *autostrada*. The main railway also runs along the coast. The Maremma is unblessed by any of the cultural centres of Tuscany, it is ill served by estate agents. Rural accommodation far from the coast is cheaper than in the province of Arezzo. The coastline itself is here at its most attractive - and the sea is reputedly clean, there being no large urban centres until Rome. But seaside villas in fashionable resorts such as Monte Argentario, where Suzanna Agnelli, of the Fiat family, was the mayor, are phenomenally expensive. The same is true of Elba. Both are popular with affluent Romans. If you must live by the sea, you are likely to get rotten value in Italy.

In spite of the mass invasion of tourists every summer and the buying up of country property, there is very little resentment against foreigners in Tuscany. True, Florentines, who had been slow to appreciate the rural beauty on their doorstep, are now upset that the prices are high. But most will admit that it was their own fault in the first place. For decades you could have bought a large Tuscan farmhouse for the price of a car. Now, no longer.

Crime in Tuscany, and throughout central Italy, is not widespread and is generally confined to the cities. There have been kidnappings in Tuscany, often organised by the Sards, but these are now rare. The most noted criminal phenomenon is probably the gruesome serial killer known as the "Florence Monster". He may have been responsible for more than a dozen killings over nearly 20 years, invariably young couples courting in cars, camp sites and so on. This maniac apart, Tuscany is a peaceful place. There is no *mafia* or *camorra*, and there is a general level of honesty. The local public administration, in the hands of the Communist Party throughout central Italy, is remarkably clean compared with both North and South.

Italian literature, after a brief flowering in Sicily, was evolved in Tuscany: Dante came from Florence, Boccaccio from Certaldo and Petrarch from Arezzo. Among Italians, there is a well recognised Tuscan character. Regarded as terrible blasphemers, Tuscans are notorious for their sarcasm and quick wit. Recently a Neapolitan friend bought some alabaster in Volterra. Throughout the customary negotiations he made a complete nuisance of himself, grovelling for discounts with the woman shopkeeper in an almost unseemly fashion. When matters were settled, we all chatted amiably enough. The woman, who had accurately identified my friend as a southerner, apparently congratulated me on my Italian. Only when we were out of the shop did my friend begin to suspect that the congratulations were not directed at me at all, but at him, a clumsy Neapolitan provincial making a good effort at speaking *la dolce lingua*. The fact that he was not certain served to increase his agony.

Although natives of Tuscany will let you forget that Italian is really their dialect, they speak the language in a most peculiar manner. Foreigners who have learned their Italian elsewhere will find it strange that locals pronounce *cosa* (thing) and *camera* (bedroom)˙as *hosa* and *hamera*. A joke is to make a Tuscan ask for a Coca-Cola with a straw: *una hoha-hola hon una hannucia*. These aspirated sounds are sometimes difficult to decipher, but ask a Tuscan to speak proper Italian at your peril.

Towards the south-east of the region, around Cortona, one is back in the land of the hard C, and Umbria is not far away.

UMBRIA

For several years now Umbria has been the "coming place" of Italy, a cheaper and less crowded alternative to Tuscany, which it geographically resembles. It is also regarded as something of a poor relation. The car number plates of Arezzo, in Tuscany, have the initials AR, which are known in Umbria as *arrivano i ricchi* (the rich are coming); in contrast Perugia's number plates are PG, or *povera gente* (poor people). Certainly Umbria has not had quite such a glorious past as Tuscany, and none of its cities have set the pace of European culture. However, with Assisi, Orvieto, Spoleto and Perugia, there is no call for condescension either. Whereas Tuscany managed in the past to go its own way, Umbria has always been under the dominance of Rome. Just as the region early formed part of the ancient Roman Republic so too, from medieval times until 1860, it was part of the Papal States. Whereas central Tuscany has rolling hills, which are capable of being cultivated under the plough, Umbria is slightly higher and the hills given over to woodland. There are steeper valleys and more water, with the Tiber running through the middle of the region. The most characteristic feature are the vast shady forests, from which Umbria may take its name (*ombra* is shade in Italian). If you like what estate agents term "mature gardens" this may well be your kind of place - although the trees go on for miles, providing shelter for an abundance of wild life, including boar (*cinghiale*). Outside the

Tiber valley, and the levels before Foligno, the agriculture is less rich than in Tuscany. There are no large wheat fields or expanses given over to vines. The horticulture is varied, with a lot of vegetables and fruit being grown. Nuts are also cultivated on a large scale. The general impression is of a land which is greener and slightly steeper than Tuscany. It is far smaller, 8,450 sq km with a (falling) population of 775,000. It is divided into only two provinces, Perugia and Terni.

Umbria is a more rural and slightly less exciting place than Tuscany. In the past, and even today, it has the reputation of being a bit of a backwater. But it gains from having a pleasant, provincial atmosphere, in the best sense of the term, and the people are friendly and unaffected. Foreigners living in the region repeatedly praise the hospitality of their neighbours. Like the more remote areas of Tuscany, there is very little crime. The only burglary I heard of involved sheets, plates and cutlery being removed. Clearly some thief was about to set up home. This is very different to near Florence, where one woman owner of a holiday home said she was considering *trompe-l'oeil* furniture.

Property prices are considerably lower in Umbria than in Tuscany. There are several reasons for this. Whereas Tuscany has traditionally attracted foreign visitors and residents because of its cultural associations, Umbria has not. Perugia, the regional capital, though an attractive city is not in the same league as Florence which, apart from its cultural associations, has several international industries on its doorstep. More important, however, are the poor communication links in Umbria. The airport serving the north of the region is Pisa, while the south looks to Rome. Neither is particularly convenient, which would be a drawback for foreigners wanting to fly over for long weekends to holiday homes. *Superstrade* do follow the Tiber down to the A1 Rome *autostrada* to the south, but Perugia to Rome can easily take three hours. Città di Castello, Umbertide, Perugia, Todi and Terni are on a main rail link to Rome, as is Orvieto, on the Florence-Rome line. The prospect of Perugia becoming an international airport is an interminable subject of discussion. The latest plans suggest that this will occur in 1990 to take some of the traffic off Rome during the World Cup. It is a case of wait and see, but if the airport does open property prices in the area will certainly rise.

The arrival of foreigners in large numbers is recent - few go back further than 1984/85 - but already their interest has pushed property prices up. Jim Powrie, an estate agent based in Umbertide, estimates prices are rising by about 30 per cent a year. In the past, property in the south of Umbria, around Orvieto, Terni, Todi and Spoleto, used to be significantly more expensive. The market was mainly driven by interest from Rome. Now with concentrations of foreigners in the north of the region, Powrie reckons prices have caught up. But he said: "Ultimately, property prices depend on the vendor. One farmer will want L50 to L60m for a house, another will want L100m. It also depends on the state of the house, which always varies."

According to Powrie, there has recently been a vast increase in Italian interest in Umbrian property. Milanese and Romans are beginning to buy on a large scale. Similarly, Italian investment houses have been asking estate agents in Umbria to ear-mark estates and large rural houses which may be suitable for investment. This interest, as well as no evidence yet that purchasers from abroad are slowing down, means that the property boom in Umbria goes on - at least for the moment.

Nonetheless, according to estate agent prices, which constitute the international market, prices remain lower than in Tuscany. The following details selected from 1989 listings give some idea of the type of property available and prices. On a hilltop near Umbertide with "magnificent views", a ruined farmhouse which "requires major remedial works", is for sale at £8,800; in the Niccone valley, between Mercatale and Cortona, in Tuscany, a large stone farmhouse, with two-storey detached barn and some land, is priced at £26,500; a "wonderful old farmhouse" near Città di Castello, with barn suitable for conversion into a three bedroomed house and two acres, described as "camping habitable", was for sale for £50,700; a fully restored farmhouse near Petrelle, with four bedrooms, kitchen, dining room, study and sitting room, cost £95,000.

Much of the recent popularity of Umbria in Britain is due to John Tunstill, an estate agent based in Città di Castello and in Gloucestershire. Tunstill is immensely skilled in the art of public relations. As a result of his efforts, various journalists have been enticed to Umbria and there has been a flood of articles in newspapers, magazines and TV programmes. The result has been a mini-boom in Umbrian rural property, which for decades has been regarded as practically valueless. There are now quite high concentrations of foreigners around Città di Castello, Umbertide, Perugia and south towards Todi. It must be stressed, however, that the greatest number of "foreigners" in Umbria are Romans, who have weekend homes in the region.

The area around Lake Trasimeno is now so popular with the British that it has been dubbed "Trasimenoshire" by the local press. *Umbria* magazine, which comes out with the Florence newspaper *La Nazione*, estimates that around 300 Britons live near the lake. It interviewed Nigel Jamieson, a music critic for *The Times*, who has lived in Castiglione del Lago, on the western shore, for six years with his wife, Alison, also a writer and an expert on international terrorism. Jamieson was quoted:

> "We arrived in Trasimeno at the end of 1983. At first we wanted to find somewhere in Campania, along the coast, but the prices were prohibitive and, besides, we could only have bought into a condominium set-up. So we thought about lakes and came to Umbria. Until two years ago Umbria was completely unknown to most English. Perugia was a name just about known, although not precisely where it was. Nobody had heard of Gubbio or Todi. Only Orvieto was well known, perhaps because of the famous painting by Turner. Then suddenly everyone in England began talking about Umbria, newspapers, magazines, television. Estate agents opened branches: in Castiglione del Lago there are already two and soon they will not have anything to sell, so great is the demand, and certainly speculative building will begin. Everything has happened so fast that we feel rather shaken. We, let's say of the old guard, were hardly a dozen. Now there must be around 100 English people in Trasimeno, even though, for the moment, the majority come only for holidays with the intention of living here permanently as soon as they retire. I do not know whether it is good or bad. Certainly it is a small invasion. The fundamental difference between us

and the new arrivals is in age and motivation. We were all young, who decided to live in Trasimeno as a choice in life."

In the same feature an Italian journalist, Luciano Festuccia, analysed the development. He suspected that the supposed end of internal frontiers which may occur in 1992 would transform Italy into a "European Florida" and the English, "who understand colonialism well", are setting the pace for the rush to the sun. But he too wondered whether new arrivals, particularly those who have retired, would successfully adapt to local society.

"There is a difference between the 10 or so English families - all young - who years ago moved to Trasimeno, integrating perfectly with local life. The most recent wave is composed of persons at least one generation older, in whom is typically found that reservation and cultural attitude which do not make it easy for them to learn another language or try to enter into a different social set-up. This could lead them to form their own exclusive society and not have anything to do with the locals, except when needing services. One is dealing with a too recent phenomenon to analyse it well. But one benefit, and it is considerable, has certainly been achieved: the revival of almost all the rural area of Trasimeno. That in itself is not a little."

Only time will tell whether fears that Umbria will be over-run by thousands of British pensioners are well founded. I would guess not. To enjoy Umbria, or rural Tuscany, an effort has to be made to enter into the local society, learn the language and make friends. Otherwise it will be a lonely place. Developers may buy up derelict convents and estates, turning them into international complexes similar to those found in Spain. But the appeal will be limited. Umbria is a quiet place, attractive to those wanting peace, privacy and a place in the country. It is unlikely to appeal to anyone unprepared to make some effort to enjoy it.

The best shops, schools and hospitals are all to be found in Perugia, which is situated in the centre of the region and is easily accessible. It is quite a cosmopolitan city and the seat of Italy's only Foreign University (*Università italiana per gli stranieri*). The university attracts students from all over the world for courses on Italian language, literature and history of art. Anyone thinking of living in Umbria and wanting to brush up their Italian would find it an excellent place to study. Courses are organised throughout the year.

Umbrians feel no resentment against the foreigners who have arrived in the countryside. Locals feel rural property has little value and many of them have long since abandoned the countryside for the towns. Indeed, many think that new blood from outside is a very positive influence, which can only bring a wider cultural understanding to a rather sleepy and marginal area of Italy. At the village of Preggio, for instance, where there is a large German population, locals have insisted that elementary lessons be given in both Italian and German to encourage bilingualism at an early age.

One Umbrian I spoke to, who runs a riding school near Umbertide with a Scots lady, said he could not understand this passion for broken down houses in the middle of nowhere. Forty years ago, he said, there was hunger and deprivation at Preggio and everyone had been pleased to leave. I suggested that it was beautiful and tranquil. "So is the Sahara beautiful and tranquil," he replied.

LE MARCHE

Comparatively few foreigners live in Le Marche (The Marches), although thousands descend every summer on its crowded coastal resorts, such as Rimini and Riccione. Indeed, the Italians dub Rimini the "Teutonic Caldron". The geography of the coastline is very similar to north-western Tuscany: a long strip of sand, backed by pine forests and marshes. In the past it was a neglected, malarial area, but with the post-war fetishism for sea and sand it has boomed. Thousands of holidaymakers from the industrial centres of the North charge down the A14 *autostrada*, which runs along the coast of The Marches, heading for resorts on the beach. In 1989, many were disappointed when they got there. The whole season was upset by the algal bloom in the Adriatic, which was particularly concentrated on the coast of The Marches. Hoteliers in Rimini have been particularly vociferous in demanding government compensation for a disaster which they attribute, probably correctly, to pollution from the Po. In normal years, the coast is packed, often by people with families. It is Italy's equivalent to the Spanish *costas*. The coastline becomes slightly more interesting south of Ancona, where there are rocks and sand around Sirolo.

Almost all the accommodation on the coast comprises of modern apartment blocks, and the overall effect is an ugly, crowded sprawl. To give an indication of prices in the summer of 1989, a sixth-floor flat near Civitanova Marche on the coast, with three bedrooms, living room, kitchen, two bathrooms, small balcony and large roof terrace cost £49,000. The flat had heating, but no parking.

Accommodation of this sort is greatly sought after by Italians wanting holiday homes. Foreigners are less interested in buying homes on the sea. They are attracted to the hinterland, which is similar to Umbria. Until very recently, The Marches were ignored by estate agents catering for foreigners, and even now few have houses on offer there. As a result, many regard The Marches as the "coming place" of Italy, Umbria by now having arrived.

It must be said, however, that The Marches are even more isolated than Umbria. Getting to Rome, from the north of the region particularly, would be a lengthy undertaking; Pisa even more so. Most roads link up with the *superstrade* going through Umbria, but there is the coastal A14 *autostrada*, and this will shortly join the A24, which cuts through the Abruzzi to Rome. In the south of the region, the Via Salaria, which is in part dual carriageway, passes through Ascoli Piceno to Rome. Until, or unless, the airport at Perugia opens up to international traffic, commuting for long weekends to a villa in The Marches is not very practical. There are, however, charter flights to Rimini during the summer. Rail links to Rome are poor, although you can get from coastal towns up to Bologna and the North quickly.

The Marches could well appeal to those who want to set up home in central Italy and get very good value for their money. It is an area which would have to be explored without much assistance from foreign estate agents (see p.172). While the countryside is often lovely, prices away from the coast are low. One agent recently offered a modern four-bedroomed villa, close to the Umbrian border, with living room, bathroom, kitchen, garage, gardens and balconies for £36,500. A four-to-five-bedroomed farmhouse near Amandola, north of Ascoli Piceno, which was partly restored, was priced at £15,900. A huge Papal villa was on offer for £182,000, a refurbishment grant of between £87,000 and £130,000 was available from the local comune, and the estimated costs for refurbishment around £217,000. A small town house of three bedrooms, described as "seedy but very sweet" by the agents, was priced at £9,800.

There are no big cities in The Marches and its provincial centres are little more than market towns: Ancona, Ascoli Piceno, Macerata and Pesaro. From Ancona there are passenger ferries to Yugoslavia and Greece. The region has fewer artistic treasures than Umbria, although the Renaissance splendours of Urbino go a long way to make up for the deficiency. Urbino has a well regarded university and is one Italy's most beautiful cities. Less noted, Ascoli Piceno is also a pleasant town.

The Marches have a population of only 1,350,000, and are given over almost entirely to agriculture. The Marches, from which the region is named, were formed in the eleventh century. The Papacy's grip on these lands was firm and it lost them to Italy only in 1860 when the Piedmontese army began its bloodless stampede to Naples, joining Garibaldi.

If swift communications are not a priority, then The Marches are well worth looking over.

ROME AND LAZIO

Rome and the region around it, Lazio, has the second highest concentration of foreigners in Italy. Finding accommodation in the centre of Rome can be a miserable experience. Not only are prices prohibitively high, but there is very little property available. In 1989, the *Corriere della Sera* estimated that prices in central and exclusive areas had gone up by 50 to 70 per cent in 12 months. Many people who actually have to live there find it a worthwhile arrangement to rent flats in the city and buy a home elsewhere, say in Umbria. Often flats are rented out to foreigners at, comparatively, very good prices. Landlords live in fear of having a sitting tenant on their hands because, under Italy's liberal tenancy laws, they can never get them out. The result is probably not what the legislators intended. Italians who come to the city and find a job, are not so lucky with accommodation. No one wants to let accommodation to them. It is less risky for the flat or house to remain empty. Foreigners are a better bet - although some landlords stipulate that you cannot have a residence certificate, which would give you tenancy rights. Foreigners are favoured because they generally do not stay for long and, if there is trouble, they are easy to evict.

For those who do want to buy property in Rome, there are a few bargains worth investigating. Any old block of flats which has no lift is unattractive to Italians: carrying shopping up six floors in August is burdensome. Also unpopular are first floor flats in narrow streets which get little light, a lot of noise and car fumes. Most areas of historic Rome, even the poorer ones, are pretty expensive these days, but the Ghetto is worth checking out and so is the area around Santa Maria Maggiore. The area around Termini station and the university is central, but a little squalid. Providing you have no aversion to low life and a bit of noise, it could be a convenient place to live - and certainly more interesting than the dreary, respectable areas which are miles from the centre. Sadly, Trastevere, once a very poor part of the city, has been relentlessly trendified. Youths from outside of town descend on the local bars and roar their dads' BMW convertibles around the piazzas to the admiration of assembled *ragazze*. For many who live in Trastevere its charm is wearing thin.

The estate agents and assorted house-finders who advertise in *Wanted in Rome*, a free classified advertisement sheet which comes out every fortnight, are likely to deal in deluxe dwellings. There is no substitute for slogging around the *quatiere* that appeals to you, talking to locals and putting the word out among friends.

The following figures are based on prices in Rome in May 1989 (thousands of lira per square metre) provided by Nomisma and published in the *Corriere della Sera:*

	Exclusive areas		Centre		Semi-centre		Periphery	
	Min	Max	Min	Max	Min	Max	Min	Max
New or restructured houses	4.543	6.900	4.675	7.413	2.550	3.650	1.575	2.108
Older buildings, but liveable	3.767	5.766	3.600	5.567	2.170	3.110	1.470	2.030
Restructure required	3.217	5.167	3.100	4.800	1.800	2.610	1.092	1.500

These prices reflect a recent development on the Italian scene. Rome is no longer the sleepy, backward town where what passes for government in Italy is carried out. Now, with the development of hi-tech industries along the Tiburtina valley, Rome is the third industrial city in Italy after Milan and Turin. It feels far more pushy and dynamic than it did in the past.

But for all its new wealth, Rome remains an extremely civilised and pleasant place to live, although jaded foreign correspondents occasionally vent their frustrations with 2,000-odd angry words along the lines that the Eternal City is about to fall to pieces. It is true that the traffic has become appalling. Even in mid-summer you can suffer cold-like symptoms caused by revolting fumes disgorged from the traffic. Unlike London there is little breeze to clear the air and the streets are high and narrow. There is a growing realisation even among Romans that the use of the car must be limited and curbs are expected to be introduced by the comune.

Once you have fought through the traffic and escaped from the city the countryside around Rome is spectacularly beautiful and it is not far away. Commuting is, however, not a practical option for most people as public transport is too unreliable. Buses into Rome are not feasible except in the very early hours of the morning. There are many places outside the city where express and local trains pause before coming in, but their timing is erratic. Only those who need to come to Rome occasionally should chance it.

North of Rome, Lazio, or Latium, has a wild beauty and is surprisingly empty. There are pleasant towns, which are attractive and historically interesting, such as Sutri, Capranica and Caprarola. Around the lakes, Bracciano, Vico and Bolsena, there are the usual leisure activities and newish expensive villas. Prices for property seem reasonable, however, given the proximity to Rome. South of the capital, the Alban hills, around Frascati and Castel Gandolfo, are more developed and expensive. Further south still, the countryside around Latina is seriously agricultural, given over to vegetables and fruit. The area used to be the Pontine Marshes. The coastline is extremely fashionable, particularly around San Felice Circeo (Circe's island) and villas here are as expensive as Monte Argentario in Tuscany. Again the sea, being at a distance from Rome and Naples, is reputedly clean. Sabaudia is a curious little town, a Fascist showpiece to the Duce's marsh-dredging efforts hereabouts.

There is little to the east of Rome, apart from Tivoli, site of the Renaissance Villa D'Este and Hadrian's Villa. A few miles further out begin the Abruzzi, which rise sharply to appreciable heights. Until the *autostrada*, the Abruzzi were virtually an impenetrable divide between western and eastern Italy. One's predilection for rustic simplicity and solitude would have to be intense to put up with living in these mountains for long.

The provinces of Lazio are: Frosinone, Latina, Rome, Rieti and Viterbo.

MILAN AND LOMBARDY

Milan is the centre of Italian commerce and industry. It dominates northern Italy as it always has done, except when it was challenged for a while by Venetian expansion on *terra firma*. Lombardy has the most concentrated population of all the Italian regions, about 8.5 million. In and about Milan, about 40 per cent of Italy's GNP is produced. Pluck any one of Lombardy's provincial capitals at random - Bergamo, Como, Cremona, Mantova, Milano, Pavia, Sondrio and Varese - and you will find they are among the world leaders in one sort of industry or another. Sleepy Como, for example, produces *one third* of the world's total silk.

Not surprisingly, Milan is the most expensive city in Italy to live in. A decent apartment in the centre will be beyond the reach of most, and living on the periphery can be miserable. Whereas in Rome, it may be possible to find older apartment blocks, without lifts or porters, where prices are reasonable, in Milan this is very difficult. The Brera area of the centre was once quite neglected, but now it has been much trendified. It is almost hopeless - so great are the costs - to dream of working in Milan while living in a pleasant villa on either Lake Como or Maggiore. These drawbacks are likely to be more acute for those with families.

In northern Italy, all the roads lead to Milan. Five *autostrade* feed into the city and several dual carriageway *superstrade*. It is also linked by rail to the main cities. As a result, many people choose not to live in Milan, but commute in from smaller towns and cities nearby. Unlike in Rome, the trains are quite efficient. An area popular with the British, where a bit of green can be found, is Arese, towards Lake Maggiore.

The few attractive parts of the Lombard countryside are highly sought after and extremely expensive. The unattractive Lombard plain, which resembles Kansas, is unlikely to hold many attractions except for agrophiles. Young, professional-ish people with no commitments often love Milan. It is a fast, dynamic city with a flashy social life to match. There are estimated to be about 7,000 British people in Milan.

PIEDMONT

It is a peculiar irony of Italian history that the province which united it was the least Italian of all. Nobody in the Renaissance would have considered Savoy, and thus Piedmont, part of Italy. Its institutions and culture were firmly within the ambit of France. French was spoken at the court in Turin down to Cavour's day. Turin itself has often been likened to Berlin, or was when the latter was still standing and undivided. Its streets are long and straight and there is a nineteenth-century formality about the place which hardly seems Italian at all. Whatever its aesthetic shortcomings, and with Italian cities it has immensely strong competition, Turin is not nearly as unappealing as its reputation. Those who work in it prefer it to Milan. It has since 1899 been the seat of Fiat: *Fabbrica Italiana di Automobili Torino*.

As in much of northern Italy, there is little of leisure in Piedmont, except the organised variety such as skiing. It is not the ideal place for a rustic retreat. Turin's climate is notoriously cold and wet. But for those whose affection for Italy has its limits, and who like to remain close to France, the Piedmontese countryside and weather improves south of its capital and it may be worth investigating. It will, in any case, be better value than Liguria. Unlike Lombardy, the countryside has fairly gentle hills, until you reach the higher mountains north of Genoa. The north and west of Piedmont are mountainous, these being the Alps (Piedmont = foot of the mountains).

The provinces of Piedmont are Alessandria, Asti, Cuneo, Novara, Torino, Vercelli and the Val d'Aosta, which is an autonomous region, and has a degree of self-government.

LIGURIA

Liguria has long been a favoured international watering hole. To live well here one needs money - even so, many choose the area because they have not enough for a villa on the *Côte d'Azure*. Expensive though the Italian Riviera may be, prices are still higher over the border. It is a fashionable area and it has been well trodden for many years. If you are looking for an old farmhouse to refurbish, you will be lucky to find one in Liguria. Even if you do, the chances are that it will be high in the mountains, which rise sharply from the coast, where winters can be quite harsh. Many of the more picturesque villages have long been given over to tourism and have high populations of foreigners, who arrive during the summer months.

Geographically, Liguria is a thin, coastal region which extends from the French frontier, past Genoa and meets with Tuscany just south of La Spezia. These two cities, along with Imperia and Savona, are the provincial centres of the region. Historically, the region was dominated by Genoa, whose

maritime republic rivalled Venice. Just as the latter flourished in
the protection of its lagoons, so Genoa prospered cut off from
the turbulent hinterland by unpassable mountains.

The most popular areas are the attractive coastal towns, such
as Alassio, San Remo, Savona and Ventimiglia, which has Sir
Thomas Hanbury's once wonderful gardens at La Mortola.
South of Genoa, are the resorts of the Riviera di Levante,
Portofino, Sestri and Rapallo (home of Ezra Pound and Max
Beerbohm).

The more prosperous Milanese, and similar, now flock to
their villas in these resorts on summer weekends. Sad to say,
they possibly no longer include many Genoese. Genoa itself is
in something of a crisis. Its prosperity has long rested on smoke-
stack industries, which in the past decade have been in crisis. It
has now forfeited its place as the third industrial city of Italy to
Rome. There are attempts to revive the port with a container
trade to rival Hamburg or Rotterdam. Attempts are also being
made to expand tourism. Efforts are being made to celebrate in
1992 the anniversary of the discovery of America by its most
famous son, Christopher Columbus. There is in Genoa a trace of
Merseyside, but without the spiritual death. It is very sad.
Woefully under-appreciated - its historic centre is well worth
visiting - Genoa is staggeringly impressive if only for the fact
that it has developed at all. With very little level space, factories
and offices climb up virtually sheer hillsides. The *autostrade*
which circle the city, carried by huge pillars and connected by
tunnels through the mountains, impress even those least
susceptible to such marvels of engineering. Sadly, the current
stagnation of Genoa's industries, and its difficulties in
developing new ones, is having a woeful effect on the whole
region. Liguria's population is 1.8 million, but it is falling fast as
people leave for jobs in Piedmont and Lombardy.

The price of property, while generally high, varies according
to its proximity to the coast and fashionable resorts. A few
examples may be helpful. A modern villa "2.4km from the
border", between Ventimiglia and Menton (in France), with a
view over the sea, garden, three double bedrooms and
bathrooms, living room, studio, kitchen, two terraces and solar
panels was on sale for £517,800. Another villa, again modern,
five minutes from Ventimiglia with good views, three

bedrooms, two bathrooms, balconies and terrace, garages and cantina cost £228,700.

Liguria is well served by transport services. Both the *autostrada* and railway go along the coast. Tuscany is easily reached, as are Milan and Turin. Genoa is an international airport, and there are even more flights from Nice, which is nearby.

Among Italians, the Genoese have an unfortunate reputation for being tight with money. Telling someone not to be so "Genovese" is rather rude. Incidently, the legendary meanness of the Scots has also captured the imagination of the Italians, and has entered the language.

THE VENETO

The Veneto is the only region of Italy which rivals Tuscany in the splendour of its treasures. Verona, Vicenza and Padua are cities of major cultural importance, and then there is Venice itself. Neither the countryside nor the climate compare well with Tuscany, however. From Padua down the Brenta towards Venice, the land is flat and is either given over to intensive horticulture or has small factories. There are splendid villas on the banks of the Brenta, which were the summer refuges of the Venetian aristocracy. The Villa Pisani at Stra was where Hitler and Mussolini first met in 1934. Occasionally these villas are sold, with many conditions to maintain them as historic monuments, but seldom with any change from £1 million or so. Around Verona and Vicenza, the city of Palladio, the countryside is more interesting, and likely to have a greater appeal for foreign purchasers. Villas nestle on top of small hills surrounded by cypresses or deciduous trees and the gardens are well watered. It is a beautiful although highly populated corner of Italy. For many years after the war the Veneto was the least successful region in the North and its main importance was in agriculture, particularly vines. Soave, Valpolicella, Cornegliano and Bardolino come from this region. In the past 20 years industry has expanded rapidly. Benetton, for example, is based in Treviso. The Veneto now feels very prosperous indeed, with shops selling luxury goods in all the provincial centres.

Being so close to major cities in the North, there has been none of the rural depopulation experienced in central Italy. Prices are high in the picturesque areas of the countryside. Lake Garda is less crowded and more accommodating than the lakes nearer Milan to the west.

For all its attractions, the Veneto has a far harsher climate than Tuscány. In winter it is often wet and very cold. The freezing mists which clear Venice of tourists in December and January and add to its sad beauty, are less appealing outside the city. There is snow most winters. But communications are excellent, with international flights to Verona, Treviso and Venice. The road north, out of Italy, is the excellent *autostrada* which goes over the Brenner before Innsbruck. The Veneto has a population of 4.1 million and the provinces are: Belluno, Padova, Rovigo, Treviso, Venezia, Verona and Vicenza. The people of the Veneto have a reputation for being extremely religious and even bigoted. They are also well known for their honesty.

One of the principal charms of Venice is that in spite of the masterpieces of architecture which greet the eyes virtually wherever you look the city is not a museum. It still lives, various small industries go on and working men unconnected with the tourist trade gather in bars to ask for an *ombra*, a "shadow", which is a glass of wine, so called from the days when wine sellers gathered in the shade of the campanile of St Mark. This aspect of Venice, possibly more apparent in winter months, is in danger of disappearing. The native population of the city has fallen from 180,000 to 50,000 in only 20 years. The average price of an apartment is L300 million, say £150,000. Many locals cannot afford the prices and so leave the city, where their families have lived for generations, for the dreary sprawl of Mestre. Foreigners with artistic tastes move in, and are blamed for the ruin caused.

Contessa Teresa Foscari Foscolo, a descendant of doges and a leading worthy of the Italia Nostra heritage group, said:

"We are in danger of becoming a stage without actors, a scene without a people. The foreigners, in some ways, have done too much for us in terms of restoration. One almost feels we were better off when we were poorer and there were more Venetians."

This may be unfair. A friend who works in the Venice prison, the most attractive and sought-after in Italy, prefers to commute to work from his modern flat in Treviso rather than live in the city. He says he would feel too cut off, not just geographically. The tranquility and timelessness of Venice, which persists in some areas of the city in spite of high summer's 50,000 tourists a day, has, he feels, little relevance to modern life. To the despair of his friends, who would love somewhere to stay in Venice, he feels his future lies elsewhere.

The Trentino-Alto Adige is a separate, semi-autonomous region within the Veneto with a population of 800,000. Until 1918, it was part of Austria and German is widely spoken. The two provinces are Bolzano (Bozen) and Trento, which is where the counter-Reformation Council of Trent took place. The mountains here are very high and usually under snow in winter. Friuli-Venezia Giulia is the most underestimated area of Venetia. East of the heartland of northern Italy, it neighbours Yugoslavia and southern Austria. The Dolomites have their passionate admirers, although in winter they are harsh. The population is 1.2 million and the provinces are Udine, Trieste, Pordenone and Gorizia.

EMILIA ROMAGNA

Emilia Romagna has some of the most beautiful towns in Italy and the most monotonous countryside. The region itself is modern, founded only in 1860 when the various independent states which then existed were swept away. The name comes from the great road, the Via Emilia, built by Marcus Aemilius Lepidus, one of the Triumvirate who, with Mark Anthony and Octavian, governed the Roman world before it became, under the latter, an empire. The Romagna is the ancient name for the area now made up of the provinces of Forlì and Ravenna. Apart from Ravenna and Ferrara, all the provincial capitals lie on the road, which runs from the Adriatic to Milan: Bologna, Forlì, Modena, Parma, Piacenza and Reggio nell'Emilia. There was no historical continuity between the cities, however. After a period of independence, Bologna, seat of Europe's oldest university, came within the Papal States; so did Ravenna; Ferrara fell to Venice; Piacenza and Parma were absorbed by Milan; while at Modena the Farnese established a dynasty whose founder was the son of a pope.

On the northern side of the road are endless flatlands of wheat and other crops. To the south are the beginnings of the Apennines, which are seldom over 2,000 feet, and the border with Tuscany. Here it is well worth looking for rural property. Valleys are wide, and therefore not too steep, and there are many rivers and streams. Some valleys are given over to crops and grazing, while others are thickly wooded with oaks, chesnuts and acacias. There are many small villages, called *borgate*, which are built on hillsides to save cultivatable land. Roofs are frequently not tiled but covered with stone splits. Down the Reno valley between Bologna and Pistoia, in Tuscany, runs a picturesque railway, the *Porrettana*, which passes the nineteenth-century spa of Porretta Terme.

Property is well priced, given its convenient location, between Florence and Bologna. The sad truth is that it is not a fashionable area. Indeed, an estate agent who specialises in rural property could think of no British residents who lived there. Nor was there much interest from outside Italians. The main reason is that neither the geography nor the climate are quite as agreeable as Umbria or Tuscany. The Appenines here mark the divison between Mediterranean Italy and the North. On the south-facing slopes, towards Tuscany, a few olive trees are still found; but on the north slopes to Bologna there are none. Geographically, the countryside is not quite as soft as Tuscany and Umbria. It is more rocky, with misty woodlands and fast flowing streams. Winter would be a bit cooler than in Tuscany.

Prices match these conditions. An eighteenth-century villa, with masses of room, a cottage and 17 hectares of land, including a cherry orchard, is on sale for £180,000. It needs renovation work, but is still lived in. A cottage in sound condition with two bedrooms, kitchen, living room and two storage rooms which could be converted, all in the province of

Bologna, cost £13,600. A large *casa colonica* requiring refurbishment would be priced at between £20,000 and £30,000.

Bologna is the capital of the region, an extremely prosperous and well ordered, bourgeois city, as befits what has been for many years a show-case of Communist efficiency. Of Italy's provincial cities, Bologna is one of the most comfortable to live in and the small foreign community which lives there is very loyal to it. The city stages the international book fair, many important exhibitions and has a fine opera. To live close to Bologna, should ensure that life does not become dull. Apparently, the comune has not until very recently encouraged tourism. I am informed that this is for aesthetic reasons. Bologna also has a rich gastronomic tradition, of which *spaghetti alla bolognese* may not even be a part. (I am assured that it was invented in Britain or America, as any Bolognese could tell you that a meat sauce is better with noodles than spaghetti.) Sangiovese and Lambrusco come from Emilia Romagna.

The Italian left has strong roots in Emilia Romagna. The vast, highly profitable farms on the prairies required a disciplined class of waged farm workers. There was no tradition of peasant owner-occupiers here. Country people lived in buildings which resembled barracks and, in the late nineteenth century, the Italian Socialist Party quickly gained support. During the war, the partisans of Emilia Romagna were numerous and effective. The film director, Bernardo Bertolucci, set his Marxist epic *1900* in this region along the Po. Strangely enough, Mussolini was born nearby at Predappio, in the province of Forlì.

Communications in Emilia Romagna, whose population is about 3.8 million, are excellent. There are regular flights to Bologna from Gatwick, and a very fast network of roads. Florence takes just over an hour.

CAMPANIA

Campania takes its name from the Roman province of *Campania Felix,* which was the *Côte d'Azure* of its time. Here wealthy Romans retired for the summer months to their luxurious villas, and vices. On Capri, Tiberius's *Villa Jovis* can still be seen and there are the remains of many others around Baia, in the bay north of Naples. Here Hadrian died, and Agrippina was murdered by her son, Nero. Here too, Caligula built his bridge of boats in response to the prophecy that he could no more govern Rome than he could drive his chariot across the water between Baia and Pozzuoli. Augustus died in the region, at Nola.

In more modern times, the kingdom of Naples was the last stop on the Grand Tour in Italy. Here the young English *milordi* could escape the eyes of their tutors and relax from their studies. Recreation was not without its dangers, however, John Evelyn, who visited the city in 1645, mentions that his companions went off to find the notorious courtesans of the city and "did purchase their repentence at a deare rate, after their return" by catching the pox. In spite of the presence of even more lethal diseases, Naples still has a vast population of prostitutes, including its famed transvestite *femminelle*. Soliciting women thoughtfully wait beside signs saying *prostitute vere*, real prostitutes.

The city has long attracted British visitors and in 1817 the *Gentleman's Magazine* estimated that 400 families lived here. Lady Blessington began her *menáge à trois* with Comte d'Orsay at Naples; Sir William Hamilton was British ambassador for many years, joined by his young wife Emma, who later became the mistress of Nelson. The Victorians on the whole disapproved, particularly that crashing bore Dr Arnold of Rugby, who was disgusted at this "country of fiddlers and poets, whores and scoundrels". The end of the kingdom of Naples in 1860 reduced the city to provincial status and in time the foreign visitors diminished. These days tourists visit either Pompei and Herculanium or head for the coast at Sorrento. The city, which among many other things has the finest collection of Roman sculpture in the world, is sadly ignored.

Coming from the north by train or on the *autostrada*, Naples does not look promising. The periphery is the vast, disorderly and frequently squalid sprawl around Vesuvius. Towns like Aversa, Pomigliano and Casoria are alike in their ugliness and all are permeated with the influence of the *camorra*, as the Neapolitan mafia is called. But for all the squalor, no part of Naples is ever dull and there is a sense of life and vibrancy lacking in the northern towns. With its palaces, grand *piazze* and boulevards, one can understand why Stendhal described the city as "the only capital of Italy".

For all its reputation, Naples is not universally poor. There are those who eke out miserable lives in the basements of the city, the notorious *bassi*. But the rich are very rich indeed and prices of property in the better areas of town are quite staggering. For all the official statistics, the general prosperity of Italy has had its influence. A thriving black economy is estimated to produce 300 million pairs of shoes a year. Many, of course, are made by children and under-paid women, but one notices over the years that the general level of prosperity is slowly rising.

Life in Naples, and in many other parts of the South, does not fit comfortably with *sorpasso* Italy's high regard for itself. While Milan, with its advertising agencies, international fashion shows and high-tech industries, is a major player in the developed world, Naples remains on the sidelines. The people too are very different to the "European" Italians of the North, where it has long been a joke to say that north Africa begins in the southern suburbs of Rome. There are many similar, offensively meant, analogies concerning Arabs. But the comparison is false. Southern Italy has nothing in common with the puritanical abstractions of Islam. The religion here will seem odd to Englishmen, brought up to enjoy tea, scones and a little well mannered worship with the local vicar. The overall flavour is a sort of pre-Christian paganism. Statues and cults are venerated, not theology. No cult is stronger than St Januarius, who saved Naples by miraculously holding back the lava flow from Vesuvius which once threatened it. A phial of his blood liquifies in the cathedral and the excited throng cries out *il miracolo è fatto*. There are scenes of religious frenzy at the church of the Madonna dell'Arco during Holy Week. Flagellants come bloodied and bare footed from country areas, choruses of old ladies wail alarmingly and a few of the congregation hurl themselves on the church floor and lick it.

In their domestic arrangements the Neapolitans can be equally alarming. On the morning after their marriage some neighbours of mine hung out bloodied sheets on their washing line to proclaim the wife's virtue. Admittedly, this was in a backward part of town.

The major problem with life in Naples is the crime. House-breaking is frequent and many apartments have doors made of steel. Cars and motorcycles are routinely stolen, and foreigners find it wise to own unpopular makes, right-hand drive Vauxhalls and similar. Crimes involving violence are rare outside the *camorra*, but friends have been held up at pistol point. The petty crime of Naples is in some ways self-regulating. Thieves know well that they must not over-step certain bounds of poor conduct which may provoke an unwelcome response. That is simply bad business. One teacher at the British Council in Naples had her car broken into, after she had momentarily parked it. Her handbag, money etc had all been stolen but so too had her irreplaceable teaching notes. She went to the local newsagent, a well known *guapo* or *camorra* mini-boss, and explained the problem. He listened sympathetically and the next day the notes were returned. At a recent dinner party a lady from Parma who now lives in Naples complained about bungling, inexperienced bag-snatchers who, after stealing the handbag, throw it away. In the past, the thieves had removed the money, but thoughtfully handed over to a nearby porter the expensive handbags and, more importantly, the hard-won identity cards, driving licences and so on.

Far worse than the petty crime of Naples is the *camorra*, like the *mafia* an unpleasant, murderous collection of thugs. The *camorra* has long since moved on from cigarette smuggling to pushing drugs, which are a big problem in Italy. But although drugs are the *camorra*'s major earner its influence pervades many aspects of the local economy. It is a brave policeman, or magistrate, who attempts to probe too closely. Violent deaths through *camorra* activity are likely to be around 300 in 1989, a figure which harks back to the sanguinary gang wars of the early eighties. Reasons for the killings are often pathetic. Two people were killed for attempting to set up one of the technically illegal bus services, which are a lesser *camorra* activity. The enterprise could not have been worth more than £10,000 a year.

Foreigners and many others in the city will never come across the *camorra*. Britons who have lived in the city for years have never witnessed a shoot-out or a *gambezzato*, a kneecapping, which daily make up the news in the local newspaper, *Il Mattino*. Seldom are the innocent, or the middle classes, involved. In spite of the *camorra*, Naples remains a pleasant, good humoured place which warmly welcomes, and often protects, the few foreigners who go there. There is none of the insincere affability, or the sense of fear, that the *mafia* generates in certain areas of Sicily. The origins of the organisations are different. The *camorra* is a local variant of urban crime which is occasionally controlled, whereas the *mafia* represented law and, occasionally, order in much of rural Sicily. Harold Acton, the historian, attributes the rise of both institutions, along with many other evils, to the collapse of the Bourbon kingdom of Naples (or kingdom of the Two Sicilies as it was called in 1860). There is some truth in this. The restraints of democracy have prevented Italy from having much success against organised crime. Bourbon despotism and Mussolini are more the language it understands.

Unless eccentric, foreigners will not live in Naples except for reasons of work. But near the city are seaside resorts which are popular with tourists and those wanting holiday homes. In the Bay of Naples are the three islands of Procida, Ischia and Capri. Procida is the smallest and perhaps the most interesting. It has been virtually ignored by international tourists, and still survives on fishing and small-scale horticulture. It is so close to the city, and not a salubrious part of it, that the sea is alarmingly polluted. Ferries regularly leave from Naples or Pozzuoli, the town to the north where Sophia Loren was born. (Pozzuoli, an ancient city which has a Roman amphitheatre and temples, is sinking into the sea as a result of seismic activity).

For all its beauty Capri is an impossible place to live and even Gracie Fields might have deserted it by now. Crowds of trippers from Naples are disgorged daily throughout the summer months and the island, which is only four miles long, is even attempting to restrict numbers. Nonetheless, villas on the island are reputedly very expensive and only rarely come onto the market. Again, being in the middle of the Bay of Naples the water cannot be that clean. The island is beautiful though. The towns of Capri and Anacapri are divided by the sheer rock-face of Monte Solaro, which now has a road. In spite of being neighbours, they have hated each other for centuries. To get an

idea of Capri during its Edwardian heyday, read Axel Munthe's
The Story of San Michele. Munthe lived in Anacapri, which is far
quieter than Capri, and his house, San Michele, with its Roman
treasures can be visited. Capri is still beautiful from afar. From
Munthe's balcony, which is perched high on the rock-face, it
seems like one of those clockwork islands: you turn the key and
all the buses spin round. Ferries arrive at Capri from Naples,
Amalfi and Sorrento.

Ischia is larger and probably more convenient, but it is not so
stunning. Whereas Capri is very popular with British tourists,
Ischia is predominantly a German destination. Again property
is expensive, and anyone owning it can easily obtain an income
from holiday lets. One local who does so is Lady Walton,
widow of Sir William, the composer, who lived on the island.
Ischia can be reached from either Naples or Pozzuoli.

The Sorrento peninsula is the other major resort near Naples.
It is squeezed between that city and the burgeoning port of
Salerno. Its sea might not be of the cleanest, although this is
hotly denied by locals who refer mysteriously to purifying
currents. The geography is delightful. The sprawl of Naples
ends at Castellammare di Stabia, where Al Capone was born,
and thereafter the road continues along the cliff-face to
Sorrento, passing attractive seaside villages. Sorrento itself has a
faded Edwardian charm and is quite busy. English beer is
served in some of the bars, as are chips, a passion of the
Belgians, who also flock there, as well as the British. The town
has pleasant bars and nightclubs, and the holidaymakers are
good fun. There are never so many of them as to rob Sorrento of
its appeal.

The more exclusive areas are on the other side of the
peninsula at Amalfi, Positano and Ravello. The towns are on the
sea, linked by a precipitous road on which one has to face
Neapolitan driving. The exception is Ravello. Spectacularly
sited on a mountain, it has lovely views over the coast below.
Adrian IV, the only English pope, lived for a while in the
Norman-Saracenic palace, now called Villa Rufolo, in the
twelfth century. Prices on the Sorrento peninsula reflect the fact
that there is considerable demand, some of it international. The
rich in Naples still like to have holiday homes here, as do
Italians from further away. For those wanting simply a view of

the sea, the resorts of the Bay of Naples represent rotten value. Its appeal lies in a mixture of stunning scenery, beautiful architecture, ancient remains and proximity to one of the most interesting cities in Europe. The area is not as fashionable as it once was, particularly Sorrento, and the prices are lower than those of the Riviera di Levante, in Liguria, which is geographically similar.

Prices for the rest of the Campania coastline are far lower, but then it is also less beautiful. South of Salerno the land is flat, past the Greek temples at Paestum to Agropoli. Thereafter, the hills descend into the sea to produce a more rocky and interesting coastline. The further away from Naples, the less people and prices of houses are generally lower. In Agropoli, for example, a three-bedroomed apartment in a modern block would cost about £30,000 to £40,000. A large modern house near the sea, with about six bedrooms, would cost around £120,000. Some seaside towns are more fashionable than others, and prices can vary greatly.

Away from the coast, the price of property falls markedly. In southern Italy, there is little or no awareness that people might actually like to live in the countryside. Prices can be anything. Many of the villages are depopulated, and farms abandoned. Obviously, the area around Naples is either too close to the city or given over to intensive agriculture and, therefore, is not very attractive. But along the Via Appia to Benevento the countryside is very beautiful. The hills are not too rocky and are mainly covered with chesnut and oak. Behind Salerno there are delightful, intimate hills which have not been spoiled by concrete constructions. This was, however, the area worst affected by the 1980 earthquake. Many of the buildings which collapsed were in a dilapidated state or were of the cheapest and worst modern type. This accounted for the high casualties in San Angelo dei Lombardi, for example. The possibility of earthquakes should be a serious consideration when buying any property in the Vesuvius area.

Communications with Naples are good. There are regular and charter flights from London and elsewhere. Unfortunately, Naples airport is a byword of inefficiency and punctual flights are the exception. Trains and main roads in southern Italy generally run along the coast. All pass through Naples. There are ferries to Palermo, Catania, Sardinia, Tunisia and, when not suspended, to Libya. A hydrofoil operates from Naples to the main resorts in Campania during the summer.

The region is divided into five provinces which are Naples, Caserta, Salerno, Avellino and Benevento.

BASILICATA

Basilicata is the poorest region in Italy. It has the misfortune of possessing only short strips of coast on the Tyrrhenian and Ionian seas. Tourism is poorly developed and the province has only low yield agriculture. The mountains, which are high and often inhospitable, have wild boar and even wolves. Doubtless the people have changed in the 40 years or so since Levi wrote *Christ Stopped At Eboli*. When Levi, a Piedmontese Jew, was exiled by the Fascists to Basilicata, or Lucania as it is sometimes known, he was appalled by the ignorance and superstition, including witches, which he encountered.

Potenza is the provincial capital. High on a hill, it is modern and not especially attractive. It does seem quite prosperous - another example of the astonishing transformation of southern Italy in the past 40 years. In winter, it is often snow-bound. Matera, which with Potenza is a provincial capital, is more interesting. In Levi's day, the locals still lived in caves. These were elaborately fashioned, often with tables, dining rooms and bedrooms. Even churches were underground. These caves are now preserved for anthropological study, and a modern town has been built above.

In the north of the region is Melfi, the first Norman stronghold in southern Italy, which has fine churches and a castle. Venosa is an attractive, isolated town. Horace was born here and modern Venosa is still dominated by its Roman past. Wellheads with lion sculptures are found at street corners and women still wash clothes together in what look like an old Roman bath house.

Potenza is linked on a branch road to the A3 *autostrada*, which runs from Naples to Reggio di Calabria. All the *autostrade* are toll-free south of Salerno. A *superstrada* runs from Potenza down to the Ionian coast, and then a main road to Taranto.

Property on the Tyrrhenian sea is slightly more expensive than on the Ionian. The latter is off the main rail and road links. Your rustic ruin in the middle of the countryside would cost very little. You would have to be a hermit to enjoy such solitude, however. A lady in Naples recently tried to sell off her ancestral pile in Basilicata for £40,000. The *palazzo* was in the middle of a town, far from the coast. It had four floors, countless rooms and some land. There was not a queue of potential buyers.

CALABRIA

Calabria has been less forgotten by history than Basilicata. From its high mountains, which are cool even in August, comes an abundance of water and on the plains Greek cities sprung up, at Croton and Sybaris, for example. The coast, as everywhere in Italy, has suffered in parts from an excess of holiday homes. But there are many attractive resorts. Tropea is the most fashionable. At sunset, one can sit on the beach and watch the volcano on Stromboli happily smoulder away. At Pizzo there is a pleasant beach dominated by a castle. Here Murat, Napoleon's brother-in-law and king of Naples, was executed after unwisely attempting to recover his throne. It is now a youth hostel. Further south still, opposite Sicily, is Scilla, of Scylla and Charybdis in the Odyssey. The Ionian coast is less well trodden, being over the mountains from the *autostrada*. Calabria is a beautiful and fascinating land and its people are a mixture of every culture which passed through the region. Near Brancaleone, for example, on the tip of the toe, the local dialect has strong Greek influences, although scholars are not sure whether this is due to the ancient Greeks or the Byzantines. In the early 1900s Norman Douglas travelled the region accompanied by his 12-year-old cockney catamite. The result was one of the best travel books written in English, *Old Calabria*.

For all its rich culture, Calabria is a land where the writ of government has been weak, or even non-existent. Brigandage flourished in the past, and still persists. At the time of writing, 12 kidnap victims are incarcerated somewhere on Aspromonte. In spite of the efforts of 400 *carabinieri* they have not been found, although several make-shift prisons have been discovered. The locals, around Locri and Gerace, know what is going on, but no one will talk. The mother of one kidnap victim, Cesare Casella, from Pavia in Lombardy, recently begged the women of Locri on their way to church to get their menfolk to release her son. Partial ransom had been paid, but the family, who own several garages, have no more.

Most foreigners are unlikely to get entangled in the *'Ndrangheta*, as the Calabrian *mafia* is called. Nonetheless, it can hardly be advised that children are brought up in a culture where this kind of brigandage is an accepted way of life. The intellectual horizons of the average Calabrese are not especially broad, although it must be said that contempt for government does not involve disdain for learning as well. Southerners are well known for the respect they afford the educated man. (Hereabouts, anyone who went to university is a *dottore*.) The question any foreigner considering a move to Calabria, or Sardinia or Sicily for that matter, is bound to ask is whether they are likely to be kidnapped. In general, the amount of trouble involved in kidnapping a foreigner is seldom worth the possible rewards. If a British child were taken, the media outcry would be immense. TV crews would pester politicians and the shortcomings of Italian government would be held up to international ridicule. There might even be a possibility that the Foreign Office would be upset. In short, the Italian government would fairly quickly be pushed to that stage where it had to Do Something. The *'Ndrangheta* know this perfectly well. They leave the big fry well alone. The newly prosperous, but not particularly influential, Italian middle classes are their favoured victims, such as the Casellas.

Calabria does have a high concentration of seaside holiday homes, flats and villa-ettes, where people like to get away from it all. Unfortunately, many others have the same idea and in no time speculative, often illegal, development springs up. The price of this type of accommodation, at least in brochures circulated in Britain, appears exaggerated.

The following, available in 1989, may give a general idea. Two-bedroomed flats in Scalea cost about £28,000. A modern villa, also in Scalea, made up of two apartment units in the familiar, architecturally unblessed fashion, cost £175,000.

Altogether, it comprises five bedrooms and bathrooms (some only with showers) and a garden. A two-bedroomed, totally refurbished town house in Scalea with views over the sea was for sale for £54,000. A secluded farmhouse near Buonvicino in need of modernisation but having a good view and six large rooms cost £33,000. There were 4,500 sq mtrs of land, olives and an orchard. A small farmhouse near Diamante, sound but requiring modernisation, with three rooms and storage and 10,000 sq mtrs of land, was on sale for £41,000. All the above villages are on the north-west coast of Calabria.

Calabria's provincial capitals are Reggio, Catanzaro and Cosenza. To get to the region involves a long drive or train ride from Naples. Those living on the tip of Calabria could fly to Catania, which has charter flights from London.

PUGLIA

"Thirsty" Puglia, to the ancients, is less attractive than Calabria. Apart from the Gargano promontory, the land rises to a long plateau given over to wheat fields and citrus fruits. For the Normans it was one of the richest provinces in southern Italy, and there are many castles and cathedrals which testify to its wealth. Thereafter it became less important, until in modern times irrigation created a revival. The coast is not especially beautiful, as there are few hills to create attractive bays. In most areas the plain simply sinks below the sea, in a rather anticlimactic meeting of the two.

Nonetheless, Puglia has a certain beauty, but one has to be patient and search a little harder for it. There are occasional woods and valleys which would be pleasant places to live. The towns are among the most attractive and interesting in southern Italy: Canosa, Barletta, Bitonto and Bari have impressive cathedrals. That of Bari is dedicated to St Nicholas (Father Christmas), whose remains were removed from what is now Turkey in the early Middle Ages. Lecce is built almost entirely in the baroque style and has impressed many, including Anthony Blunt, the art historian and spy who specialised in southern Italian baroque. Puglia also has a very curious and unique domestic architecture in the *trulli*. These are conical

houses, built out of the local limestone without any mortar. For
the roof, circles of stones are laid which gradually close at the
top. The outside is usually whitewashed, often painted with
religious and folk symbols. The origin of the *trulli* is very
ancient and they are now protected as national monuments.
Most are found around Alberobello and Locorotondo.

For many, the Gargano is the most attractive area of Puglia.
Here there are wooded hills and streams, and attractive views
over the sea. There are holiday villas and a few foreigners have
made their homes here. Prices are on a par with the more
fashionable areas of Calabria. Although Puglia is a long way
from any principal cities, it is well served by roads and the
railway. The A14 *autostrada* comes straight down the coast from
Emilia Romagna, through The Marches and Abruzzo. There is
no Naples to be by-passed, either. There is also an *autostrada*
going west to Naples. Regular ferries leave for Yugoslavia,
Corfu and Patras from Bari. There are also ferries to Greece
from Brindisi and Otranto. The provinces of Puglia are Foggia,
Bari, Brindisi and Lecce. Unlike Campania and Calabria, there is
no widespread organised crime.

ABRUZZO AND MOLISE

Abruzzo and Molise are now two separate regions and,
economically, are the success story of the South. In the 1980s
new industries moved to the deep valleys of the Abruzzo,
which now has little in common with the rest of the South.
Abruzzo and Molise have a formidable beauty, with the
Abruzzo National Park and the Gran Sasso d'Italia, the highest
mountain south of the Alps. But it is too harsh to attract many
who want to live there permanently. For those who think they
could stand it, there may be unexpected rewards. Because of its
sheer isolation many strange practices have persisted in the
Abruzzi which would be interesting to learn about. There is talk
of witchcraft continuing. In L'Aquila there is a curious
procession involving a Madonna covered in serpents of various
kinds. The towns in the region are very well run, often
spotlessly clean with good shops. Some, such as Atri, have
attractive medieval churches and ancient centres.

The coastline of Abruzzo and Molise is like much of the Italian Adriatic. It has long since surrendered its charms, which were not numerous, for the rewards of mass tourism. There is a lot of industrial development along the coast as well. In 1989, around Pescara, a bland, modern town, a small farmhouse with sea view over the village of Silvi, five rooms and 1,000 sq meters of land was advertised for £49,000. A one-bedroomed flat 2 kms from the sea coast was £27,000. Both required renovation. Bargains are unlikely along such a populated coastline. The A14 *autostrada* links the region to North and South, and the A25 impressively cuts through the Abruzzi to Rome. The journey would take about two and half hours provided there was no snow, which there frequently is in winter. In Abruzzo the provincial centres are L'Aquila, Teramo, Pescara and Chieti; in Molise Isernia and Campobasso. From Pescara there are ferries to Yugoslavia.

SICILY

The Norman conquest of Sicily shortly after the Norman conquest of England ensured that before long medieval Britons wanted their time-share in the sun. So it was that John of Lincoln became the canon of Agrigento, on Sicily's south coast; Richard Palmer rose to be Archbishop of Messina; and even Richard the Lionheart stopped off on his way to the Third Crusade to occupy Messina and Catania (his sister was the queen of Sicily). Connections between the two islands steadily weakened thereafter. Only the most intrepid grand tourists went on beyond Naples, although by the end of the nineteenth century it had become quite fashionable. It became considerably more so in the 1900s, when both Kaiser Wilhelm and Edward VII visited the island. Taormina was particularly popular with single gentlemen until, in Harold Acton's words, it became "a polite synonym for sodom". In Marsala a quite different British community became established. In 1773 John Woodhouse shipped local white wine to Liverpool, conserving it by adding more alcohol. So began the taste for Marsala wine, an alternative to port and madeira. Soon other traders joined in, notably Ingham and Whitaker. Marsala bearing these names can still be bought, although the establishments have been owned by Cinzano since the 1920s.

These days there is no British community as such in Sicily. Many British subjects who have married Sicilians live on the island, and there are quite a few at Palermo and Catania. Others work for the oil companies at Gela. Those who live there say Sicily's reputation is undeserved, just as the Irish say Ulster is not as bad as the television would have you believe. One English woman married to a Sicilian says she feels freer living in Sicily than she did in England, in Yorkshire. Sicilian women go to university and possibly more continue to work after having children than is the case in England.

But another picture of Sicily emerged in 1989 when a 19-year-old Sicilian writer, Lara Cardella, won a magazine prize to publish her novel *Volevo i Pantaloni*, I Wanted To Wear Trousers. Cardella, who lives in Licata on the south coast, tells the story of a young girl growing up in provincial Sicily. It is unhappy reading. As the girl grows up care-free childhood gives way to an adolescence of ever diminishing horizons. Oafish and predatory males restrict her freedom at every turn. As a teenage girl she cannot even walk down the streets of her town eating an ice-cream without brain numbing vulgarities being shouted after her. In short, Cardella depicted a petty, mean and backward little world for which she obviously felt profound contempt. The novel caused a sensation in Italy and quickly shot into the best seller listings. But the people of Licata were mortified. In a TV interview the mayor of the town said the book was based on the fabrications of a psycologically disturbed mind. To show that they were not mean and backward, but members of a tolerant western democracy, people in Licata staged a hate campaign against Cardella's family. Her mother fled her job at the local hospital in tears and the youthful author found it prudent not to leave home for a few days. When she did venture into the piazza she was reviled as a *putana* who had disgraced the town. Not without cause, the Italian press has dubbed Cardella as "Salman Rushdie in a mini-skirt". I discussed the book with an English woman who lived in Catania. She thought it was exaggerated and described conditions which existed 20 years ago. For a 30-year-old woman from Palermo, now living in Rome, it was entirely convincing.

The description of a young woman taunted for eating ice-cream on a Sicilian street seemed to her spot on.

Sicily has many virtues which compensate for its vices. It is breathtakingly lovely in parts and the impress of great civilisations makes it one of the most interesting corners of Europe. The coastline is spectacularly beautiful, particularly in the south where the fast currents between Sicily and north Africa keep the water astonishingly cool. Palermo is a fascinating mixture of beauty and macabre. Wonderful Norman-Saracenic and baroque churches contrast with the occasional - sometimes not so occasional - *mafia* killings. The Capuchin catacombs, where the fully clothed skeletons of the "illustrious corpses" of past city dignitaries are still on display is pure Vincent Price. Sadly, Palermo closes down at around seven in the evening and everyone flees for home.

Syracuse is more relaxed and very beautiful. It has many ancient remains, as befits what was once the second largest Greek city after Athens. Cefalù is an attractive Norman town on the northern coast and Taormina, on the slopes of Etna, looking over the sea, is delightful. The view through the Roman theatre, where performances still take place in summer, is much celebrated. Bronte, on the west slopes of Etna, was the seat of the dukedom bestowed on Nelson by a grateful King of Naples and his heirs sold the estate only in 1981. When an impoverished, but bright Ulsterman won a scholarship to Cambridge he decided Bronte was a good enough name to adopt. His literary daughters carried it to greater fame.

It is easily possible in Sicily to own a holiday home anywhere on the island. It is possible to live there permanently as well. But whether one would want to bring up a family on the island, and become absorbed into the local life as many British people have been in Tuscany and Umbria, is more questionable. The *mafia* must be a major consideration. It undermines the quality of life of so many people; for a minority it ends life altogether. In northern Europe we are perhaps over-governed and Italy seems delightfully anarchic and free. In Sicily the lack of government is not freedom, it simply provides the opportunity for thugs to act as they please and push everyone else around. To experience the kind of ambience a heavy *mafia* presence creates, a few days spent in Corleone should do the trick. Very suitably, the town gave its name to the family in the *Godfather* movie. In the early years of this century, Corleone lost more than 100 citizens in a *vendetta* lasting several decades. Alcamo too is another *mafia* infested small town. A few incredibly brave people, and they are mainly Sicilians, do try to fight back and limit the *mafia*'s awesome power. The most celebrated is Giovanni Falcone, the investigating magistrate behind the huge "bunker" trials in Palermo. This summer a bomb containing 60 kilos of gelignite was left near his villa - enough to flatten everything for 100 metres. Fortunately it was discovered by one of Falcone's 24 permanent bodyguards. If there is such a thing as the living dead, it is Falcone. The thinking in Palermo is that it is only a matter of time before the *mafia* get their man. The best book on the *mafia*, and essential reading for anyone thinking of living in Sicily, is Norman Lewis's brilliant *The Honoured Society*.

There is no British-based estate agent specialising in Sicily, so investigations will have to take place on the spot. Prices will be high on the east coast around Taormina, which at Easter hosts Rome's *glitterati*. It is served by the airport at Catania. The northern coast is better linked with roads and has more tourists, mainly other Italians. This is beginning to mar the beauty of Cefalù. The west of Sicily, beyond Palermo, towards Trapani and Marsala, are cheaper. Best of all is the south coast, where there are fewer main roads or cities. Agrigento, the third largest city of ancient Greece, has fine archeological remains. For holiday flats, prices are generally lower than Calabria, but not by much. Local conditions decide the rural property market. The price for a farm is based on what the land is worth. The difficulty will be in finding someone to assist you in purchasing it without robbing you blind. Good luck.

There are international flights to Palermo, and ferries from Naples, Genoa, Livorno, Cagliari (Sardinia) and Tunis. From Syracuse you can get boats to Malta and Tripoli. From Agrigento there is a ferry to the island of Lampedusa, the most southern territory of Italy. Sicily's provincial centres are Palermo, Trapani, Messina, Agrigento, Caltanissetta, Enna, Catania, Ragusa and Siracusa.

SARDINIA

At Porto Cervo did Aga Khan a stately pleasuredome decree. Here, on the Costa Smeralda, are concentrated the splendid villas of the international rich. The coastline and sea here are staggeringly beautiful and, under these circumstances, the prices of villas seem quite reasonable. The appeal of much of the south of France and Marbella is less obvious. Prices vary markedly, depending on whether bath taps are gold or the hall is fitted with Joan Collins-style marble and brass accoutrements. One villa on the Costa Smeralda, with three bedrooms and two large terraces at the end of a beach was advertised for only £230,000 ono. Perhaps the occasional kidnapping keeps the prices down.

Anyone who can afford a lifestyle on the Costa Smeralda is likely to know a good deal more of what it would entail than the author. Other parts of the coast also have holiday complexes of a more modest nature. It can be fairly said that one does not buy this type of property in order to get to know the locals, or because of any particular fascination for Sardinia. Those who feel that the effort would be rewarding can find traditional property at low prices.

For most people, however, Sardinia is a place to spend a holiday, not to bring up a family. The values of the islanders reflect centuries of peripheral government and limited horizons. So far as law and order are concerned this is Sicily, but without the money or the subtlety.

If you are not arriving in Sardinia by private yacht, there is an airport at Cagliari, which has international flights. Italian internal flights land at Olbia and Sassari. Ferries operate to Civitavecchia, Naples and Genoa. From Olbia there are ferries to Civitavecchia, Genoa and Livorno. The provinces are Sassari, Oristano, Cagliari and Nuoro.

3 Italy: Past and Present

THE BEGINNINGS

Present day Italy is an incomprehensible place without some idea of how it came into being. Travelling the length of the peninsula, it sometimes seems that you are passing through a succession of different countries. As a nation state Italy is very young, unified only in 1860, but Italian culture is ancient and venerable. The fragmented city states which made up the peninsula, although small and militarily to be proved weak, were among the main players in European history. Indeed, in the late middle ages and then the Renaissance, the Italian cities set the pace of European culture.

All the present nation states of Europe - England, France, Spain, Germany and Italy - owe their origin to the tribal migrations which destroyed the Roman Empire and continued after its fall. With the retrospect of 10 centuries or so, the history of England seems smooth, simple and almost planned. Angles, Saxons, Danes and the indigenous Celts were moulded together by their Norman conquerors, so producing the "English". The frontiers of Norman England were little different to the borders of today. Since 1066 there has been no successful invasion of England, nor has there been the same degree of sweeping change shared by all the rest of western Europe during the French Revolution.

There is no such clear evolution into a nation to explain Italy. The destruction of the Roman Empire did not end civilisation in the peninsula entirely. The Dark Ages were less dark in Italy

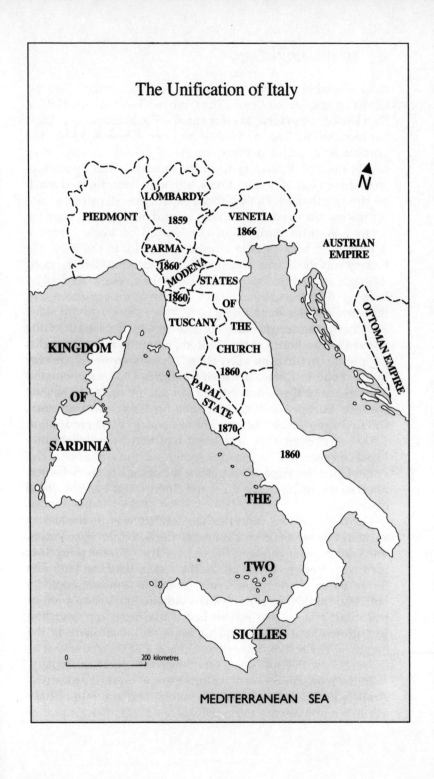

The Unification of Italy

PIEDMONT

LOMBARDY
1859

VENETIA
1866

AUSTRIAN
EMPIRE

PARMA
1860

MODENA
1860

STATES
OF

TUSCANY

THE

CHURCH
1860

PAPAL
STATE
1870

OTTOMAN EMPIRE

KINGDOM

OF

SARDINIA

1860

THE

TWO

SICILIES

0   200 kilometres

MEDITERRANEAN   SEA

than elsewhere. Some conquering German tribes became Christian and settled down. The tomb of Theodoric the Goth, a Dalek-like structure at Ravenna, is testimony to their sophistication. The arrival of a later German tribe, the Lombards, changed matters. Unlike previous invaders, they totally rejected Roman institutions and laws. The Byzantines were driven out of northern Italy, although they still held much of the South and Sicily. Through all this disruption one institution survived: the Papacy, even though at this time the Pope was little more than the bishop of Rome, itself a depopulated backwater in a turbulent world. In the West, the Papacy was the one legitimate source of authority which traced its origin, as *pontifex maximus*, back to the Caesars. As well as keeping alive the Christian faith, the Papacy represented law, literature and the Roman ideal.

Charlemagne, the king of the newly Christian Franks, revived the authority of the old Roman Empire to legitimise his conquests. On Christmas Day 800AD, he was crowned emperor by the Pope in Rome. It would be difficult to exaggerate the importance of this event. More than any other, it established western Europe, and its influence on Italy was profound. Charlemagne's Holy Roman Empire was to exist for another 1,000 years. Even more important was that by insisting on a Papal coronation, Charlemagne recognised the authority of the Pope. Later the Pope would claim the authority to make and unmake the rulers in the West and Empire and Papacy would clash.

For the next two centuries the conflict was postponed as western Europe again succumbed to the barbarian invasions of the Vikings, Magyars and Saracens. Parts of Italy went their own way. Venice, which unlike the rest of northern Italy was never under Charlemagne's rule, looked to Constantinople for both trade and cultural motivation. Amalfi, like Venice a refuge from barbarians, also established a maritime republic. The Byzantines kept Puglia and Calabria, but lost Sicily to the Saracens. The rest of Italy fell into chaos. The Papacy was at its lowest ebb, with Popes being set up by rival Roman factions.

In the eleventh century western Europe revived again. The Arabs were kept behind the Pyrenees, and the raids of the Vikings and Magyars eventually petered out. The Empire of

Charlemagne had survived, but in a reduced and weakened state. What is now France had its own king and Britain had several. But Germany and Italy were bound to the imperial idea, the universal state which claimed authority over all western Europe. The result was that national feeling could not crystallise around their own distinct rulers.

An upsurge of religious feeling at this time transformed the Papacy, providing it with much of the authority it was to possess throughout the Middle Ages. All western Europe acknowledged the Pope's power. Inevitably, the Papacy clashed with its only possible rival, the Empire. Ostensibly, the quarrel began over the appointment of bishops but it accelerated into something much greater: which institution was to preside over the fortunes of Christendom. Did Church serve state, or did state serve Church?

The cities of Italy, which during the preceding centuries had become partial to independence, were pawns in the conflict which was to last more than 150 years. Towards the end of the eleventh century, the emperor marched on Rome. The Pope turned in desperation to the only force in Italy which could defeat the invader: the Norman brigands, who were busily carving dukedoms for themselves out of lands belonging to Lombards, Byzantines and Saracens. The Normans drove back the emperor, and spectacularly plundered Rome, causing more damage than the earlier barbarians. As a result of their efforts, the Pope recognised Norman rule and the kingdom of Naples (southern Italy and Sicily) came into being. This was a crucial event for the future of Italy.

By the end of the eleventh century, Palermo was the most populous city in western Europe as well as the most interesting. Under Norman rule Arabs, Greeks and Jews were governed with an exceptional degree of tolerance and the kingdom prospered. At the end of the century, the Papacy crowned all its achievements by launching the First Crusade, which saw the successful conquest of the Holy Land. The brains of the enterprise were in large part the Normans from southern Italy and Bohemund, their chief, made Antioch capital of a new duchy.

At this time, southern Italy was more prosperous and better governed than the centre and North. Strong cities, particularly

Milan, were vehemently pro-Papacy or, more specifically, wanted freedom from the heavy hand of imperial subjugation. Florence too was an anti-Empire stronghold. Smaller neighbours, Cremona and Siena for example, would in turn seek protection against them from the Empire. The two sides were soon to be called Guelfs, the Papal party, and Ghibellines. The cause of the conflict soon became irrelevant for the Italian cities. They joined which ever side best served their parochial interests.

The Papacy had won immense prestige. Every king in Europe acknowledged the Pope's authority, while in Italy imperial power was in retreat. That the conflict did not end sooner, with the emperor retiring north of the Alps, was due to dynastic accident. The Norman royal family in southern Italy married into the German emperor's. The result was that in the thirteenth century Frederick II became emperor of Germany and northern Italy, and king of southern Italy too. For the Papacy, which was surrounded and vulnerable to imperial interference, this was a disaster which it had struggled hard to avoid. Worse still was that Frederick II was one of the most remarkable rulers of the Middle Ages. Brought up in semi-Arabic Palermo, Frederick was to prove a highly cultured and ruthless defender of what he considered imperial rights. Contemporaries called him *stupor mundi*, the wonder of the world, on account of his extraordinary abilities. Campaigning through Italy, he would travel accompanied by his Saracen bodyguards from Sicily and a caravan of camels carrying his harem. Over 30 years, Frederick came close to subduing northern Italy and bringing it firmly under imperial authority. This was in spite of the Papacy launching repeated crusades against him and issuing several excommunications.

After Frederick's death in 1250, the Papacy wreaked a terrible revenge. It decided to end forever the German presence in southern Italy. With the help of the French, it ensured that all Frederick's heirs were ruthlessly killed. This was deemed, by Dante among other, to be one of the more repugnant crimes of the Middle Ages.

The death of Frederick, and his heirs, marked the end of southern Italy's prominence. The future belonged to the cities of the North and centre, which were now free from the threat of imperial rule. Some cities were already powerful, such as Milan. As usual, Venice went its own way, avoiding involvement in the Papal-Empire struggles and generally enriching itself. Its maritime empire had increased in strength ever since 1204 when the city diverted the Fourth Crusade from going to the Holy Land and directed it instead to looting Christian Constantinople. This act of appalling faithlessness shocked even contemporaries. There is not a slab of marble on St Mark's that was not stolen from the Byzantines, Venice's long standing trading partners. Genoa and Pisa were the *Serenissima*'s poorer rivals.

In literature too the future lay in the North, with the vernacular of Tuscany. Written in the early fourteenth century, Dante's *Divine Comedy* is, among other things, a sad critique of contemporary Italy written by an embittered exile from Florence. Riddled with factional conflict and jealously competing commercial cities, Dante felt Italy was politically corrupted. He longed for a return of the Empire, with its legitimate authority and order. And he thought the Pope should occupy himself primarily with spiritual matters. It is Boccaccio, writing slightly later, who better catches the mood of the age with his lewd and profane tales about the fast money middle classes. Early humanism is expressed by Petrarch in poetry which marked a break with the medieval past.

Dante's hopes of a revived Empire were hopelessly unrealistic. Even the power of Frederick II had depended far more on his Sicilian kingdom than on anything he possessed north of the Alps, where the title of emperor was virtually an honorific. In the absence of imperial power, petty dynasties grew up in the city states of northern Italy: at Milan there were the Viscontis; at Mantua the Gonzagas; at Verona the Della Scala. In Tuscany, Florence, Siena and Pisa remained republics. For much of the fourteenth century even the Papacy's baleful influence on secular politics was absent from Italy. The now French-dominated curia had moved to Avignon.

THE MIDDLE

The first half of the fourteenth century was a period of great prosperity and progress in Italy. There was a sharp reversal in fortunes after 1348 when the Black Death struck Europe. Siena lost about a third of its population and its grandiose cathedral was never·to be finished, as can be seen today. Florence too suffered badly, although even before the plague it was in financial crisis caused by Edward III of England not repaying his debts. For all its savagery, the Black Death created only a pause in Italy's development. The North was still the richest and most populous area of Europe. Only the Low Countries, which were also urbanised, came close to rivalling its wealth. The fifteenth century saw the city states of Italy reaching the peak of their achievements. Whether the Renaissance was a development of the Italian Middle Ages, or whether it did represent a decisive break with the past, as the great nineteenth century historian Jacob Burckhardt believed, is still warmly disputed. What is beyond doubt is that there was an intellectual ferment in the states of northern Italy which was quite different to anything that was going on elsewhere in Europe. The old medieval order of Empire and Papacy, for all the theory, had provided neither law, order, nor even moral authority. The Italian cities had made their own way, sending their merchants throughout Europe and the Middle East, and the result had been spectacular success and wealth. With wealth came leisure, and speculative thought. Intellectuals looked back to the past, to the republics of Greece and Rome, and found there values which owed nothing to Christianity. Secular thought, dormant for 1,000 years, began to re-emerge. Man was the measure of all things, in art as in politics.

Nowhere was this new learning more keenly felt than in the wool manufacturing and banking city of Florence. Under ostensibly republican institutions, the Medici governed unobtrusively and presided over the cultural revival. The rest of Italy, particularly Rome and Venice, also made major contributions to the Renaissance. The 100 years between 1450 and 1550 were the finest in Italy's history. Never again was she to be more influential and admired. In architecture, painting, sculpture and literature, Italians set the taste of Europe. When

Galileo disproved the idea that the earth was centre of the Universe, it must have seemed that every truth preached for centuries by the church was under threat from the new learning.

Even in Italy's finest moment, however, two events occurred which were to have catastrophic consequences for the peninsula. The most obvious to contemporaries, such as Macchiavelli, was the successful invasion of Italy by the French king to enforce dynastic rights in Naples. This event was to presage countless wars in the land and result in foreign domination that continued until unification. The other event was more serious. In 1492 Columbus sailed the ocean blue. This signalled the end of the Mediterranean as the centre of world trade and with it the pivotal role of Italy was to diminish. It is a great irony of history that America was discovered by an Italian, albeit employed by Spain.

By the beginning of the seventeenth century, Italy's relative prosperity was beginning to decline and cultural life stagnated as the Papacy imposed a disciplined and assertive theology on the Catholic church to fight against the Protestant menace in northern Europe. Through inheritance and conquest, silver-rich Spain now possessed southern Italy and Milan. In the titanic clash between French Bourbons and the Austro/Spanish Habsburgs for the mastery of Europe, northern Italy was to be the preferred battleground. In time, only the Papal States and Venice were to remain independent. Alessandro Manzoni's classic *I Promessi Sposi* (The Betrothed) is set in and around Milan during this period of poverty and recurrent war. By the time British grand tourists arrived in the eighteenth century to see the sights and buy a few cut-price old masters, Italy was one of the poorest and most backward areas of Europe. The Age of Enlightenment, which saw such great figures as Newton, Locke, Voltaire and Herder, had hardly an echo in Italy. The country seemed given over to priests and the parochial. The French Revolution was to change everything.

THE UNIFICATION OF ITALY

In 1789 the political arrangement of Italy was little different from medieval times. Milan and Lombardy were no longer ruled by Spain but by the Austrians. After centuries of independence they had returned to being a fief of the Holy Roman Empire. Tuscany too was under Austrian control, ruled by the Lorraine family. The Papacy and Venice, the two hardy perennials of Italian history, remained independent although, in the case of the latter, now a weak echo of its former power. The *regno*, the kingdom as the South was called, had its own dynasty of Bourbons. The kingdom of Savoy, with its capital at Turin, had also survived throughout repeated occupations and wars. It was, however, the least Italian of the states in the peninsula. Its territory straddled the Alps and included parts of what is now France. French was spoken at its court in Turin and its institutions were based on French feudal arrangements. Few Italians would consider it Italian at all. Ironically, it was to lead Italy to unity.

In 1796 the armies of revolutionary France crossed the Alps. Under Napoleon, then a republican general, the French swept the Austrians out of most of northern Italy and set up satellite republics. Feudal institutions which had survived the repeated conquests by traditional states, were deracinated. In time the revolutionary armies invaded the Papal States and took Naples, where they set up the short-lived Parthenopean republic. Venice too was taken, ending 1,000 years of independence. Throughout the Napoleonic wars, only Sicily remained free of the French, protected by the British fleet under Nelson. Napoleon, as a good quasi Italian (his family was supposed to have come from San Miniato in Tuscany), parcelled out the principalities of Italy to members of his family. When the Pope objected to the despoilation of the Papal States and excommunicated Napoleon, he was imprisoned. Naples was handed over to Murat, the swaggering cavalry general and Napoleon's brother-in-law. Although he managed to eject the British from Capri, Murat failed to invade Sicily. Earlier, the British and French had clashed in Calabria in a small and inconclusive battle at the village of Maida. Hence, Maida Vale in London.

Napoleon's disasters in Russia resulted in his brothers and sisters having to seek alternative employment and the Italian possessions returned to the conservative rulers who had possessed them 20 years before. As well as Lombardy, the Austrians directly governed Venice, the Republic of St Mark had disappeared for good. Murat alone attempted to save his throne, rallying support by advocating the unification of Italy. This was the first time this growing sentiment was expressed by a serious ruler in Italy. Sadly, the Austrians easily defeated Murat and deposed him. In an episode of sheer folly which occasionally characterised his actions, Murat attempted to reclaim his throne by staging a Napoleonic return in Calabria. Unlike his master he did not take the precaution of landing with 1,000 armed men. He was ignominiously shot.

The French under Napoleon were perhaps not the ideal liberators of Italy. As well as freeing Italians from feudalism and the dead hand of clerical rule, the French also liberated many of Italy's most precious treasures. Even the lions of St Mark found their way to Paris. But in spite of this, the republican-Napoleonic occupation was of immense importance to Italy, and Germany. There was a surge in national feeling in both countries and this, rather than liberalism, was to be the lasting legacy of the French Revolution. In the crises of the twentieth century it was to be these youngest states in Europe which were to turn to fascism.

In the 1830s the idea of a united Italy gained currency. Initially it was confined to republican-democratic sympathisers. Stendhal's *Charterhouse of Parma* brilliantly evokes these times, in which repressive and obsolete petty states tried to stifle emerging national, democratic feeling. The great theoretician of Italian unity was Giuseppe Mazzini, a Genoese who was exiled from Italy when only 25. For most of his life he lived in London, where his dark good looks led to him being much fêted by drawing room patriots. However, as well as being an indifferent ideologue, Mazzini was an appallingly incompetent revolutionary. Any plot that he had a hand in was assured of complete failure. So irrelevant did he become, that monarchic Italy found it no threat to proclaim him as one of the three great architects of the *Risorgimento*, the resurgence.

After several disastrous plots, one of which, in Parma, involved the Anglo-Italian *Risorgimento* martyr Enrico Misley, the outlook for a united Italy improved with the revolutions of 1848. The wave of uprisings which convulsed Europe began in Sicily and soon the peninsula's rulers were showering democratic constitutions on their subjects. Although the republican patriots seized control in Venice, under the able Daniele Manin, and in Rome, under Mazzini and the adventurer/matinée idol Garibaldi, another power began to challenge the liberals' assumption that they would unite Italy. The House of Savoy, which governed Piedmont, had long proved themselves formidable survivors in one of Europe's most dangerous frontier states. Their state, at that time called the Kingdom of Sardinia, was made up of French and Italian speaking subjects. In an age of nationalism it was fast becoming an anomaly. To silence the noisy Piedmontese democrats, the king declared war on the Austrians who were having difficulties holding Lombardy and the Veneto after the revolutions. Sadly, the ancient Marshal Radetzsky soundly defeated the Piedmontese liberators. The patriots in Venice and Rome fought on heroically, but were eventually defeated. The old regime, and the Austrians, returned.

The events of 1848 showed that there were two roads to Italian independence: either under what was now a constitutional monarchy in Piedmont, or under the leadership of the republican patriots. The propertied classes everywhere in Europe were beginning to lose their appetite for revolution. No longer could it be confined simply to civil rights and parliamentary government. Revolution would now inevitably involve an element of social reform. Many of the middle classes felt safer supporting Piedmont. Many confined their protests against foreign rule to witty snubs. After performances at La Scala opera house they would chant the name of Verdi to the confusion of their Austrian rulers. The great composer's name was an acronym for *Vittorio Emanuele Re D'Italia*, Victor Emmanuele being the king of Piedmont.

The third and brightest of the three architects of Italian unity now came to the fore. Mazzini and Garibaldi were no match for Camillo Cavour. At best a lukewarm Italian patriot, Cavour realised that Piedmont had to change with the times. He also understood that conservatives would have to lead the movement for Italian unity if it was not to get out of hand with Mazzini and his dark-eyed republican conspirators. Completely cynical, Cavour would have been quite happy if Italian unity had simply extended Piedmontese control over northern and central Italy. The impoverished, backward South had limited attractions to him.

A point which Cavour quickly grasped, and Mazzini never did, was that to free Italy of the Austrians would require outside help. In 1859 he made a thoroughly unscrupulous deal with Emperor Napoleon III, who was always looking for adventures abroad in order to live up to his over-large name. Cavour agreed that if Piedmont was attacked by Austria, France would come to her aid. In exchange, Piedmont would cede French speaking Savoy to France and Italian Nice. This shameless arrangement nearly broke the heart of Garibaldi, who had been born in Nice, or Nizza to give it its Italian name.

It remained only for Cavour to provoke war with Austria, now a visibly decaying power. This was easily done and the French/Piedmontese armies won the expected glorious victories at Magenta (where blood seeping through French blue uniforms gave rise to the colour) and Solferino. Delighted by these successes, moderate patriots kicked out their Austrian rulers in Tuscany and Umbria and Le Marche rebelled against the Pope. All northern and central Italy looked as though it would fall to Piedmont. Napoleon III had not anticipated such a vastly expanded Italian state on his southern border and so quickly made peace, before the Veneto could be freed. At Villafranca, the French and Austrians divided out the Italian states in the last arrangement of this kind which Italy was to experience. France was to receive Lombardy, but cede it to Piedmont; Tuscany and Modena were to have back their hopeless Austrian dukes; Umbria and Le Marche were to be restored to the Pope. Cavour, appalled, resigned. Other European states now intervened and insisted on better terms. Britain, particularly, wanted to see a strong Italy which might be played against France. Quickly plebiscites were held throughout northern Italy and Tuscany and everywhere the voters wanted union with Piedmont. The French-Austrian deal was undermined and Cavour returned to power.

At this moment, the long dormant democratic wing of the *Risorgimento* achieved its greatest success. In spite of hesitant support from Cavour, Garibaldi and the Thousand now landed in Sicily, exploiting local unrest. The kingdom of Naples had long been regarded as one of the worst governed states in Europe. Gladstone had whipped up outrage in Britain at the sorry plight of Neapolitan liberals imprisoned after the failed 1848 revolution. This was not a fair view. The Bourbon monarchy was certainly incompetent and occasionally brutal and repressive. It certainly never honoured any of its promises for democratic constitutions. In this it was being realistic, as the disaster encountered by liberal Italy in the South would show. But whatever its shortcomings, the kingdom of Naples did at least belong to the southern Italians. It had existed for 800 years and its king was not a foreigner. After unification the South became a picturesque appendage to the rest of Italy, almost a colony.

The triumphal march of Garibaldi through Sicily and on to Naples is the most cherished myth of the *Risorgimento*. In many ways it was a third rate farce. Fighting was slight and there were few casualties. Most of the Neapolitan government had already been bribed into betraying their king. *The Leopard* by Giuseppe di Lampedusa brilliantly portrays a terminally corrupt Sicily which accepted Italy just as it had most other conquerors. For the prince in the book, as for the rest of the southern ruling class, "everything had to change in order to remain the same".

Garibaldi's landing at Marsala was saved by the presence of British warships protecting the then British owned wine trade. The Neapolitans dared not fire near British ships. Initially, Garibaldi was welcomed by the Sicilian peasantry, but they soon realised unification would not mean great changes for them. Before leaving Sicily, the *Garibaldini* were putting down peasant uprisings in order to protect property. As Garibaldi neared Naples, its young king obligingly fled. British sailors and foreign tourists joined Garibaldi and put on the fetching red shirts of his band. Alexandre Dumas followed proceedings in his yacht. By the time Naples was reached the liberators seemed like a carnival coming to town.

Garibaldi's victories presented Cavour with a serious problem. The hero appeared intent on proceeding to Rome, which was protected by a strong French garrison. Garibaldi was now no longer on speaking terms with Cavour and refused to hand over his conquests to Piedmont. The loss of Nice to France had caused serious upset. In desperation, the Piedmontese army bloodlessly invaded the Papal States, adding Umbria and Le Marche to Italy, and met up with Garibaldi north of Naples. Vittorio Emanuele, whose statues of martial posturing disfigure so many Italian cities, arrived to be hailed by Garibaldi as "king of Italy". Garibaldi in turn was hailed as a great victor, his conquests were quickly taken over by Piedmont and he retired to his island home off Sardinia, Caprera. Annexation of southern Italy was confirmed by plebiscites, which were blatantly fixed.

Only Rome, with Lazio, and Venice remained outside the kingdom of Italy. Venice was added in 1866 when Austria was unsuccessfully fighting Prussia, which like Piedmont was leading the movement for German unification. When Bismark turned his attention to France, defeating Napoleon III in 1870, Italy seized the opportunity to take over Rome. Papal soldiers put up token resistance and the Italian army streamed through the Porta Pia, near where the British Embassy now stands. The capital of Italy, which to Turin's fury had moved to Florence, now passed to Rome. The Pope, regarding himself as a prisoner, retired to the Vatican and refused to recognise the new state. Italy, in the form we now know it, was born.

THE KINGDOM OF ITALY

The new kingdom was from the start engulfed with problems. The war in the South had caused an upsurge in brigandage and free trade suddenly introduced to the area wiped out its small efforts at industry, which were then bought up by northern speculators. When Palermo rebelled it was bombarded by the Italian navy - the same atrocity which had aroused European revulsion against the old kingdom of Naples.

Abroad the unification of Italy was considered a wonderful, romantic success. Garibaldi was tremendously popular in

Britain. Many pubs still bear his name. Contemporaries referred to his "sublime" expression and praise his "simplicity". He was, in truth, a man capable of breath-taking folly. His inability to make up his mind whether he was a monarchist or a republican is a serious detraction from his general heroism. When he came to London, there were scenes of frenzied admiration, "Garibaldi-mania". Only two people remained unimpressed: one was Queen Victoria, the other was Karl Marx.

Newly unified Italy was not a prosperous country. There was 70 per cent illiteracy and very little industry. The institutions of democratic Italy proved to be fertile ground for *mafia* and *camorra* interests. The South was utterly impoverished and for many the answer was emigration. Between 1860 and 1914 about 9,000,000 Italians left their newly unified homeland, mainly for the United States and South America. In the North, however, there were the beginnings of serious industries. In 1899 a group of Piedmontese businessmen set up an automobile factory in Turin. This was FIAT and it was another four years before Henry Ford was to set up his workshop in Michigan. Olivetti and other impressive industrial concerns were to follow.

In politics the kingdom of Italy had almost as many governments as the present republic set up after the Second World War. But although governments were often shortlived, the same old faces held office. One prime minister, Giovanni Giolitti, was in power for considerable periods and in Italy his name now defines an era. Giolitti introduced much of the social legislation of these years. As today, there were wide differences in prosperity in the country and the regions of Italy maintained the cultural distinctions which had evolved over hundreds of years. It was Mussolini who would prohibit dialects in schools and wholeheartedly encourage an Italian national character. Meanwhile, in the newly industrial North another feature of Italian politics was developing. The head of FIAT, Giovanni Agnelli, regarded himself and his colleagues as almost above government. "We industrialists," he used to say, "are ministerial by definition." Not much has changed.

Italy's foreign policy was confused before the First World War. Far too poor to be an imperial power, it nonetheless conquered a few deserts in Eritrea and Libya. Its attempts to subdue Ethiopia led to the greatest defeat, at Adowa (1896), ever meted out to a colonial power by a black state. In Europe Italy was a partner of the Triple Alliance with Austria and Germany. But it gained little from this arrangement and promptly reneged on it when the First World War began. When Italy did join the war in 1915 it was to obtain the unredeemed territories (*irredentismo*) of the Alto Adige and Friuli. Total war proved too great a strain on a country with as few resources as Italy. Its armies initially did well against the Austrians. But in 1917, with Russia out of the war, enlarged Austrian forces, stiffened up with German divisions, routed the Italians at Caporetto. Astonishingly, after fleeing across three rivers, the Italian army managed to reform and hold the enemy on the Piave. Thereafter the Austrians weakened and in 1918 the Italians sealed their victory in the battle of Vittorio Veneto.

FASCISM

The cost of victory in the First World War was immense. Italy lost 680,000 men. In the peace negotiations after the war, Italy came off badly. It had entered the war to secure its eastern border and the Trentino, up to the Brenner pass on the border with Austria. It also wanted more of Africa or Turkey, and in the efforts to involve Italy in the war these had been promised. But territorial ambitions fitted ill with the idea of President Wilson to "make the world safe for democracy". Italy did in the end win most of her demands on her European borders, but not elsewhere. While Britain had added 2.5 million miles to her empire and France a million, Italy obtained only 100,000 miles and most of that was desert. Many among the thinking classes felt the peace had been a swindle.

More serious than these territorial grievances was the fact that Italy faced social revolution after the war. The government was chronically indebted and industry was in crisis as it switched to a peace economy. Riots and strikes spread through the country and Socialism gained power. Matters came to a head when the workers occupied the factories of the North in 1920, led by Antonio Gramsci, the principal ideologue of the new *Partito Communista d'Italia*. The government proved incapable of maintaining order. Such conditions proved fertile ground for the Fascist bands of Benito Mussolini. Formerly the great hope of the Socialist Party, Mussolini was an ultra-nationalist who had vehemently supported the war. Now he and his bands, the *Fascio di Combattimenti*, called for national reconstruction, an end to the red menace and social reform. The middle classes liked the sound of this, and were even more pleased to see the Communists and Socialists being beaten up and kicked out of the town halls they had held since the end of the war. Bologna, a Communist stronghold, was particularly savagely treated. In the elections of 1921 the Fascists won 35 seats. In spite of this low number, by exploiting the divisions of his enemies and controlling the streets, symbolised by the Fascists' March on Rome, the king was manoeuvred into appointing Mussolini prime minister in 1922.

The head of a coalition government, Mussolini quickly increased his power. A change in the electoral system gave the Fascists a convincing majority of seats in 1924. In the next two years Italy was transformed into a police state. The press was gagged and opposition parties were banned. Local councils, which had been the power base of the Socialists, were replaced by nominated officials (*podestà*) and councils. Political enemies were hunted down by a secret police, called bluntly *Opera Volontaria Repressione anti-Fascista*, or OVRA.

Initially, Fascist economic policy continued the free enterprise system of liberal Italy. But in time trade unions were banned, and were replaced by Fascist syndicates. High tariffs kept out foreign competition and the fledgling Italian industry performed well. The crash of 1929 increased Fascist intervention in the economy. As banks and certain industries faced ruin, Mussolini set up the *Istituzione della Ricostruzione Industriale* (IRI) which by 1940 controlled more than 40 per cent of Italian industry. This degree of public ownership was unique in western Europe. Indeed, IRI still exists to this day, controlling about 30 per cent of Italian industry, and has led to a unique co-existence of public and private sectors. Given such control over the economy, Mussolini's attempts to make Italy self-sufficient - the battle for grain etc - had some success.

Mussolini is also credited with healing the breach with the Papacy with the Concordat of 1929. Since unification the Pope had refused to recognise the kingdom of Italy because it had ended its secular power by absorbing the Papal States. Mussolini, who was sycophantic towards the church, is credited with great diplomacy for this achievement. In fact after 50 years or so it was about time the Papacy stopped sulking and recognised one of the most important Catholic nations in the world. One bad result of the Concordat is that St Peter's is now approached along the monumental Via della Conciliazione, instead of, as was the case, through the winding streets of the medieval *borgo*.

For all the totalitarian assertiveness of Fascist Italy, it was never a ruthlessly efficient state. The trains often did not run on time. The main victims of Fascism were the thinking classes and industrial workers, who had no freedom to organise for better pay and conditions. The Communist Party leaders were purged. Togliatti, the great post-war leader, fled to Russia and now, ironically, FIAT's Lada plant is in the town of Togliattigrad. Antonio Gramsci, the greatly influential non-Leninist ideologue of the Italian Communist Party, died in a Fascist prison. Jews too were persecuted with laws which plainly aped Nazi Germany. Mixed marriages were banned in 1938, and Jews had been deprived of professional posts. The laws were not popular. Under German pressure Jews were rounded up and sent to concentration camps in 1943. A half to two-thirds of Italian Jewry, which in total was less than 100,000, was exterminated. Primo Levi, who was at Auschwitz, can be read on this subject.

Italy has escaped the opprobrium attached to Germany after its Nazi regime. That it did so owed more to the Italian people than the restraint of the Fascist state. The Italians are not a people who take kindly to government of any sort. Fascist rule, like that of its tougher predecessors, was watered down with complexities and frustrations.

Nonetheless, it is wrong to think that Fascist Italy was not an obnoxious, murderous little state. Italian armies committed atrocious barbarities in Ethiopia, using poisoned gas on civilians and machine gunning refugee camps. Marshals Badoglio and Grazziani, who were mainly responsible, were never held to account for this. Similarly, whole villages were wiped out by Italian soldiers in Yugoslavia in attempts to destroy the partisans. They can still be seen as empty ruins to this day. Internment of civilians on a large scale was also an

Italian policy in the Balkans. Neglect and incompetence, perhaps partially deliberate, meant they were never properly housed or fed and thousands died. Although more than 2,000 Italian officers and civil servants were identified as alleged war criminals, none have ever been tried.

When the Second World War began, Mussolini did not act rashly. He only declared war on June 10 1940, when it was clear France was doomed and, in all probability, Britain also. When fighting actually began, the Italian performance was everywhere disastrous. Even Greece managed to put the Italian army to flight. As hundreds of thousands of Italian soldiers surrendered in north Africa it was difficult to regard them as serious enemies. The arrival of the Allies in Sicily finished Fascist Italy. The king, belatedly seeing the danger to the throne, sacked Mussolini and then fled south to join the Allies. To everyone's annoyance the surrender of Italy did not mean an end to the war, as Hitler poured troops into the peninsula. The head of the government, Marshal Badoglio, who had surrendered to the Allies, now declared war on Germany for its unwarranted invasion. Mussolini, freed from imprisonment by German paratroopers, set up the Nazi satellite "Italian Social Republic" in the North.

While the Allied armies fought slowly up what Churchill had wrongly called the "soft under-belly of Europe", Italian partisans became an important and heroic force. In all, 36,000 were to die with another 10,000 killed in German reprisals. Mussolini was captured by partisans on Lake Como and executed in April 1945.

ITALY TODAY

Of the three Axis powers, Italy suffered the least. Her disaster-prone military efforts, early surrender and later assistance to the Allied cause created a general feeling that the Italians had not wholeheartedly backed the Fascist war effort. No city in Italy suffered the systematic destruction which was meted out to Japan and Germany. After the war, there was no equivalent of "De-Nazification" and non-fraternization. Indeed, thousands of Italian women married their liberators, GIs being far more eligible than the poorer British. Nonetheless, the Second World War had completely bankrupted Italy, its infrastructure was left in tatters and its people near starvation. Norman Lewis's auto-biographical *Naples '44*, as well as being a brilliant read, describes an Italy which is for younger people quite difficult to imagine.

In 1946 elections were held, in which women voted for the first time, and a parliament began to work out a constitution. An early casualty was the monarchy, which was voted away in a very close referendum. Two features of modern Italian politics began to form: the Christian Democrats and the opposition Communist Party. The latter, clearly enough, had impeccable anti-Fascist credentials and was popular in the North and centre where the partisans had been strong. The Christian Democrats were more ambivalent. They looked back to the Sicilian priest Don Sturzo who had founded the successful anti-Fascist Popular Party after the First World War. Christian Democracy advocated a few socialistic policies, such as representation of workers in factory administration and breaking-up the large country estates. But in general it was a new veneer for the non-Fascist, Catholic ruling groups. Not quite the Tory Party of Italy, it is nonetheless the natural party of government. Since 1946, when it took shape under its great leader Alcide De Gasperi, the DC has been part of all the 40 odd governments the Italian republic has experienced. The names of the prime ministers might change, but very little else does. Giulio Andreotti, the present prime minister and perennial political fixture of Italy - Beelzebub to his enemies - first held office in 1946 and has been in and out of it continuously ever since. No British politician has enjoyed such longevity.

The most striking feature of Italy since the war has been its phenomenal economic growth which transformed what had hitherto been a rural country. Between 1953 and 1968, Italian industrial production increased by 200 per cent, a feat matched only by West Germany and Japan. The social consequences of this expansion have been profound. Since the war 8,000,000 people have left the land for jobs in the cities. Until very recently this meant that they headed for the great industrial centres of the North. Throughout the 1950s vast numbers of impoverished southerners would make their way up to

Lombardy and Piedmont, to look for work. In Turin the reserved locals looked on the new arrivals with apprehension and a little disgust. Older Turinese, like the founder of Fiat, would refer to the new immigrants as "those Italians".

In the 1970s world recession brought the post-war boom to a halt. For a time it looked as though Italy was headed for complete chaos. Government became engulfed in debt, the economic growth halted and there were repeated political crises. Whereas Britain had the Winter of Discontent and the three-day week, Italy had the Red Brigades. Between 1975 and 1980, 27 Fiat managers were shot by terrorists and four died. Repeated strikes and sit-ins disrupted the factories. For the first time, it looked as though the Communists might win power. Gianni Agnelli, the Fiat chairman, went around with a cyanide capsule in case of terrorist capture. "Fiat makes cars with one hand and fights a guerrilla war with the other," he said in 1979. In the same year, matters reached a peak with the murder of the former prime minister, Aldo Moro. A year later neo-Fascists blew up Bologna station killing about 80 people for no obvious reason at all.

But in the 1980s Italy has again staged an astonishing recovery. Today the pessimism of the 1970s, the "Dark Days", is over, the Red Brigades are no longer active and the economy is booming. In 1986 Italy announced that it had replaced Britain as the fifth industrial power in the world. This *sorpasso*, or "overtaking", was disputed at the time. It is less so now, with the OECD recognising it having taken place. As with the prosperity of Britain, Italy's revival in fortunes is linked to the world economy, with the United States playing the pivotal role. In Britain, one might see a break with the 1970s in the miners' strike or the Falklands war. In Italy it was the mass dismissals at Fiat in 1980. Over-manned and in the doldrums, Fiat staggered through the Seventies with dwindling profits. Its managing director, Cesare Romiti recalls: "We had terrorism, drugs and prostitution in our plants. The atmosphere was pre-revolutionary." In a carefully laid plan, Fiat attempted to sack 24,000 workers over three months with compensation assisted by the state payments. This would have been astonishing in any country, even more so in Italy where traditionally it was almost impossible to sack anyone. The result was a surge in militancy, with mounting violence and dark threats against managers. For 35 days Turin was paralysed. It ended when middle ranking Fiat employees and some workers staged a huge rally in support of the company, which they thought was on its knees. In the face of such opposition the unions and Communist Party collapsed, and the job losses were accepted.

This victory for Italian capitalism did not change everything over night but it was a clear break with the past. A new confidence in business was created which spread throughout the economy. The 1980s has seen a surge in prosperity. Even the South has gained. Caserta, near Naples, has the Fiat Tipo plant which is reputedly one of the most modern in the world. Immigration to the North is no longer what it was. In 1960 about 170,000 southerners emigrated, now the figure is about 14,000. But the South is still poor. A recent study estimated that average annual earnings in the province of Enna, in central Sicily, were £3,000. This squares unevenly with *sorpasso* Italy. The *mafia* has also enjoyed a boom since the war. Mussolini is rightly credited with stamping on the Sicilian "honoured society". But another point is that criminal activity in backward 1930s Sicily was unlikely to be any more remunerative than legitimate enterprises. Sicily produced very little that anybody wanted. The big killings, in earnings and in cadavers, lay with the Italo-Americans. The *mafia* revived with the Allies' invasion of Sicily. Renowned American patriots like Lucky Luciano and Vito Genovese, who was virtually given Naples as his personal fief, were enroled as consultants by the US army. Supplying the locals with nylons, petrol, or food and penicillin proved lucrative. These days Palermo is a major exporter of heroin. The *camorra*, the Neapolitan equivalent, has a hand in many illegal pies, including running illegal immigrants, of which there are about 700,000 in Italy. The Calabrese *'Ndrangheta*, more primitive than the others, sticks to what it does best, which is kidnapping.

The 1980s has also seen Milan become a successful international business centre. In 1985-86 its stockmarket capitalisation soared from being about a tenth of the size of London to being about a fifth. At the heart of Italy's economic success are the small, often family run, industrial concerns. In 1970, when in Britain big was supposedly beautiful, only 840

Italian companies employed more than 500 workers. There is now a vast number of these small firms. Highly competitive or they disappear, they keep costs down and give an outlet to Italians' considerable entrepreneurial skills. Taken together they represent a creative and resilient presence in the economy, an invaluable national asset. Every city in Italy has some degree of manufacturing. The entire country buzzes with an energy which simply does not exist in provincial Britain. Even Naples, which is certainly poor, chaotic and crime-ridden, is not economically stagnant.

The great weakness of the country, and the secret of its success, is the abysmal nature of the Italian government. Although there is a consistency in Italian politics - the Christian Democrats always remain in power - the quick succession of feeble administrations is destabilising. Government posts and contracts are bartered away among the various factions in Rome, and there is precious little genuine civic feeling. For years no one seriously attempted to tackle the public debt, which now equals a staggering one year of GNP. Perversely, in one way the financial crisis of the government actually benefits its citizens. Second to the Japanese, the Italians are the biggest savers in the world. With exchange controls, they are unable to invest abroad and many avoid the corrupt Milan stock exchange. The result is they buy government stock, and the more indebted the government becomes the better off they are. Whether after 1992, and the freedom of capital, Italians will continue to buy government stock when they can get whatever they like at London or Frankfurt is a worry. Some analysts fear this could cause a profound crisis of confidence in the government.

Neither governments, nor law, nor the state are especially respected in Italy. The notion of Italy itself carries little weight with a people who are far more proud of being Venetians or Florentines or Milanese. In Britain it is unimaginable that a judge would be corrupt. Completely gaga, possibly, but not corrupt. In Italy this is not the case. There is no faith in government, which is often weak, partial and inept. When it attempts to do something unpalatable, it is frustrated or ignored. When Bettino Craxi became prime minister he admitted he could not find the levers of power. Power in politics and in business lies in the hands of cliques and factions - *clientelismo* - who help each other on. Often this assistance comes perilously close to what Anglo-Saxons would regard as blatant corruption. So natural is the process, however, that to point this out would almost seem a lapse in manners. There are appalling scandals. In 1982 Roberto Calvi was found hanging below Blackfriars Bridge in London. Several hundred million dollars from his bank were not so easy to find. He was almost certainly murdered. The P-2 masonic lodge scandal was another bizarre episode of the Eighties. Presided over by the fantastic Liceo Gelli, who considered himself a latterday Cagliostro, the lodge united *mafia* big shots and neo-Fascist terrorists with bankers, generals, MPs and the state security service. The aim, apart from generally carving up the spoils of power through mutual assistance, appears to have been to create an alternative government in Italy. Stronger stuff, anyway, than is to be found in the smoke filled rooms of Transport House or machinations at the Carlton Club.

Business life too is presided over by powerful groups, at the peak of which is Gianni Agnelli. Agnelli controls about a quarter of the Italian private economy. Obsequiously referred to by the press as *L'Avvocato* – "the lawyer", although he has never practised - Agnelli has a power unequalled by any other private citizen in a western democracy. Elsewhere the concentration of power in his hands would have been curbed. Those who believe in regulated, democratic free enterprise, along the Anglo-Saxon model, find Agnelli an unacceptable kind of capitalist. In fact he is more a consequence of Italy's phenomenal success than the instrument of it. Young men in striped shirts from the Harvard Business School did not make Italy what it has become today. It was achieved by necessity, to end the deprivations of war and centuries of impoverished misery. Italy has worked hard to become as wealthy as it is today, and it is rightly proud of the achievement. If one man, Agnelli, has benefited far more than anyone else, it still seems to many an acceptable enough price to pay.

There is in Italy a general collusion to keep the state weak. No one trusts it, and many gain. An astonishing number of Italians pay no income tax of any kind, and most fiddle it in a way that is impossible with our cherished Inland Revenue. In 1984 it was estimated that tax avoidance amounted to L182,000 billion - enough to pay the government's annual debt. If tax is not paid, it is easy enough to understand how regulations on safety at work, pollution, employment of minors, minimum wages and so forth are also circumvented. For the small businessmen, who are the winners in Italian society, it is a happy states of affairs. For the losers, the crowded families in the notorious *bassi* of Naples or Palermo, the victims of *mafia* violence, the appeal of ineffectual government is less obvious.

Italians are greatly excited by the prospects of 1992. They know that they cannot lose, and regard Mrs Thatcher's stubborn opposition to joining the European Monetary System as very unsporting. Few references to the British prime minister fail to remind readers that she is *la donna di ferro*. Britain is frequently described as the "Trojan horse of Europe", with its screwdriver factories owned by the Japanese. This would be more convincing if Italy was not a) a byword for restrictive practices and monopolies, and b) did not herself go cap in hand to the Japanese for investment in such alluring locations as Palermo and the Bay of Naples. For the Italians, 1992 mainly offers a huge free market for its burgeoning industry. It could also result in sound money, stable government and defence: three benefits the Italian government has not managed to provide. While other countries, which are by nature respectful to government, apply even damaging regulations from Strasbourg and Brussels, in Italy uncongenial legislation will no doubt be obfuscated, confused and generally frustrated in the traditional manner. 1992 Europe is going to be a game with high stakes, and the Italians are confident they will win it.

4 Finding a Home

Italy's "housing stock", if that prosaic term is apt, is immensely varied. Whether you are searching for a secluded villa, a fortified manor house, a dilapidated monastery, an idyllic farm or a shepherd's cottage you will find all are available. No other country in Europe contains so much architectural beauty. Old and venerable buildings, even if only poor farms, are scattered around the countryside and many have been little altered for hundreds of years. Just as the Italian landscape can suddenly change from one valley to the next, so too do the local styles of construction and the materials used to build them. As for the cities, they are among the most magnificent human achievements in the world. In spite of the motor car and other pressures of modern life, Italian cities, towns and even rural villages, have a vibrancy lacking in Britain. Indeed, to British eyes the urban centres must seem curious places. No dual carriageway runs up the Corso in Rome, an international bank has not covered the remains of the Forum, the eye-sores of multi-storey parking have been avoided - the pavements, though cluttered, do just as well - and provincial towns have not been re-arranged for the benefit of supermarket managers. In spite of the evidence that must be daily before their eyes at home, there are occasional British visitors who nonetheless feel they have something to teach Italians regarding the conservation of their heritage. This is condescending nonsense. With the possible exception of Ceauçescu's Rumania, it is difficult to think of any other European country which has tried so systematically to make itself as ugly as Britain - or shown such contempt for its past. A profoundly Anglophile friend once remarked that if Venice had belonged to the English they would have filled in the canals to make roads. It was impossible to disagree.

This does not, of course, mean that Italy is without its own version of unappealing modern developments. But urban sprawl is on the whole just that: the worst of the jerry-built, speculative apartment blocks are in new suburbs, spreading out from the ·historic centres. However grim and devoid of architectural merit these buildings may be, they do actually house the populace. The reason for the obliteration of, say, the centre of Winchester, is far less clear. The developments surrounding Italian cities also sound a familiar note, and anyone feeling nostalgic for the delights of Birmingham's Bull Ring should take a trip to the peripheries of Milan or Naples.

Of course, one consequence of Italy's frantic urbanisation has been the depopulation of the countryside. With the exception of fashionable areas, such as Tuscany and Umbria, rural property is being sold for piffling sums compared with those paid even for small apartments near urban centres. Exus Italian Homes, a British based estate agent which specialises in property in Le Marche, east of Umbria, last summer advertised a "small old house in mountain village. Needs work but could be lived in after a clean-up. Good value. Price: £10,900 L.25 million" and "interesting and attractive old house partly restored. Shady, sloping wood behind, small house thrown in. Price: £21,300 L.49 million." The significant point about these prices is that they are not exceptional. Of course, at the other end of the property market Sotheby's International Realty 1989 sold Palladio's Villa Cornaro for $2.3 million.

ON YOUR OWN

Once you have decided on the area, or areas, where you might like to live the next step is to begin the hunt for a home. Most people like to do this in June and July. In popular areas this sudden demand causes a mini property boom and decisions may have to be made fast in order to secure the property of your choice. In these circumstances it is sensible to have sufficient sums of money readily available, through arrangements with an Italian bank, in order to pay a deposit on the property. The deposit can be up to 30 per cent of the asking price and these matters are considered in greater detail in the next chapter. It could well be a better idea, particularly if you plan to live in Italy all year round, to see what conditions are like during other periods of the year. A charming cottage with pleasant soothing breezes in August may well be freezing cold, even snow bound, in winter. One acquaintance, living beside the Tiber north of Umbertide, in Umbria, found great enjoyment relaxing on his lawn beside the cooling flow of the river in summer. His wife regularly bathes in the water (to the locals' disgust). But in winter, with the incessant rains of November and March, the river level regularly rises ten feet above the garden and laps up against the back door. Empathy with the ancient river chills proportionately.

Spring and autumn are good times to look for property in Italy, as elsewhere. In winter many sellers are resolved to stay put, and hibernate for the duration. Early summer is when most foreigners set off house-hunting and in August everything stops in Italy, with vendors, *geometri* and *notaii* all heading for the beach.

Many buyers, particularly those who know Italy speak the language or have friends there, prefer to avoid the British-based estate agents who sell property in the country. They feel, often rightly, that prices will be better if they find properties for sale themselves rather than rely on international estate agents lists, with all the commissions and possible price loading that may be involved. In any case, private sales are more the norm in Italy than buying through estate agents. The difficulty is finding the kind of property you want to buy, particularly in rural areas. Before leaving to begin your quest, it is a good idea to check the classified advertisements in the British press. If promising properties are advertised they are worth investigating. Houses with rustic charm or beautiful views which have appealed to one foreign buyer could well appeal to a second. There are also many advantages in buying from a British seller. For a start, communication between buyer and seller is easier and there will be less chance of misunderstandings. More importantly, many of the financial arrangements for the purchase could take place in Britain. This practice is widespread among foreigners, although not popular with the Italian revenue, which will not know what is going on and will find it difficult to estimate capital gains.

Property is also advertised in all the Italian papers, although these will tend to be flats in cities and towns rather than *case rustiche*, which sell mainly to foreigners. Another form of advertising is for sellers to attach little pink or green signs outside their homes with the word *vendesi*, for sale, with possibly a few details of the property and a phone number. Neither method is wonderfully efficient and a lot of time can be spent desperately trying to find a home in the area you prefer - as any Roman or Milanese, whose cities suffer dire housing shortages, will tell you. To get things moving it is wise to cast your net as widely as possible. Use friends, and friends of friends, to pass the word that you are looking for a house.

It is always a good idea to speak to local estate agents. In Britain property transfers and estate agency are extremely efficient. The whole system is organised on highly commercial, possibly even excessively commercial, lines. This means that a perceptible market in property exists in Britain. Those who want to buy a three-bedroomed semi will have an accurate idea of how much they are likely to have to pay for it because thousands of similar houses are on the market, advertised by many different agents. In the spring of 1988, London property was going up a few thousand pounds every week because buyers were prepared to pay the money. This was an extreme example of how efficiently responsive the British market in homes can be. By that time ordinary residential property had become such a lucrative market that even vast organisations, such as Lloyds Bank and Prudential, had joined the game by moving into estate agency. Estate agents, and some of their clients, made substantial sums of money. Many people who now live in Italy could afford to make the move simply because they sold their house in Britain for a price beyond their wildest dreams of avarice. For those still in the UK property market it was a story with a less happy ending. By the summer of 1989 property prices had slumped and the only houses being sold in London cost 15 to 25 per cent less than the year before.

Italy's residential property market is far less market-driven. Whereas the single office estate agent is now rare in Britain, this is still very much the way the business is run in Italy. One reason for this is that Italians, in common with many other continentals, regard the frequency with which Britons change their homes with utter amazement. Buying a home in Italy, or France, involves long-term commitment to a certain lifestyle. Italians will generally want to remain in their *paese*, where they have grown up and have family and friends. The eagerness with which British people, particularly the old, seem prepared to desert their homeland and families is regarded as very odd. Traditionally, there has been little financial incentive to hop from one home to the next. Although in modern times there has been a boom in values in overcrowded cities, along the coast and in other tourist areas, in much of Italy property prices have remained stagnant, or even fallen. It was these circumstances which, in the recent past, allowed foreigners to buy up farm houses in Tuscany for less than the price of a car.

The disadvantage of the Italian property market, as it is currently organised, is that it is not at all clear how much one should pay for a particular property. Thus in Naples, where property in the centre of town is extraordinarily expensive, an apartment in one palazzo occupied by "pleasant" neighbours can cost far more than a similar apartment nearby, with less worthy neighbours. Foreigners, who are in any case outside the restrictive social norms of the city's bourgeoisie, can live relatively painlessly in a central but unfashionable part of town without suffering the loss of status which would apply to a native. For some people these considerations are extremely important.

So far as rural properties are concerned, the criteria for deciding the value of a house may also work in a foreigner's favour. The estate agent may mark a property's value down because it is far from the exciting shopping available in a modern town, and only close to a humdrum, medieval village. Similarly, the price of a country house, however hideous, may be astronomic if it is within sight of the sea. The general point applies that as there is no easily fathomable market the price of property can fluctuate wildly. This is less the case, of course, for such well trodden areas as Chianti, Siena, Lucca or San Gimignano, where the value foreigners place on rustic simplicity is now well understood. When buying property in

Italy, and much else, hard-headed negotiation with an eye never wavering from the bottom line (ie cost) is the best policy.

If you do see the house of your dreams with a private "for sale" sign outside it, you must be prepared for a good deal of haggling. In spite of their own great, but very recent, wealth, many Italians cannot quite believe that all foreigners are not immensely rich. The initial prices some private sellers demand for a property can be absurdly high - as any estate agent would tell them. Unless the seller shows some sign of being capable of reasonable negotiation it is best to give up on him and continue looking elsewhere. If the area and local ways are not known to you, it will be wise to see the property with an Italian friend who can ask the kind of specialised questions that you may not think of: is the owner seriously wanting to sell or is he a time-waster, are any of the neighbours *coltivatori diretti* who have first right to buy the property (see pp.109-12), is the land invaded during the hunting season, are the foresters about to chop down all the woods, is the comune helpful or a hinderance and so on. An important question, to be asked at this stage and checked by your lawyer, is whether the house has been built without permission (a widespread practice in the South) or illegally altered. Fines, even demolition, can result.

All rural property should also be checked over by a *geometra* (a surveyor), who can tell you what work needs to be done and how much it is likely to cost. Provided he is not connected to the seller and is not, as is often the case, an estate agent as well, he can provide a reliable assessment of the property's worth. While looking over any property try to be circumspect. Gushing praise for the view or the delightful rusticity of the house are likely to translate as millions of additional lira on the asking price. If the owner, or estate agent, is selling hard, needlessly pointing out every feature of the house or view, avoid giving the impression that you are utterly charmed. Drawing his attention to drawbacks such as damp patches, broken tiles, ill-fitting doors, may help indicate that the house price cannot be stratospheric. When you do decide to buy, you are doing so purely out of a sense of altruism rather than for any benefit to yourself. Italians are masters at this sort of thing and if you even approach their level of skill you are doing well.

If you decide to buy an apartment, you will need to be aware of the complexities of the condominium system. Generally speaking, if you buy a flat in Britain you are likely to be a leaseholder, as will all your neighbours, and the freehold of the property will belong to a landlord, or property company. In Italy, and in many other countries, matters are organised through a condominium. A condominium (*condominio*) is a joint ownership arrangement whereby the residents in a block of flats own outright their homes and jointly own with their neighbours all the common parts of the property: the land on which the building stands, the roof, outside walls, gutters, drains, corridors, lifts, lobby and so on.

There are advantages and disadvantages in a condominium. The main advantage is that the leasehold/ freehold arrangement is avoided and property is owned outright. This is an important consideration in a country where people do not move home regularly and property ownership is often as a matter of course passed down through the family. Offspring do not have the unpleasant surprise of inheriting a family home which only has 15 years or so on the lease.

The great disadvantage of a condominium is that the responsibility for running the block falls on the residents, who have to agree to the decisions made. Whereas in Britain all the freeholders have a common interest in getting the landlord to make improvements and keep things in good repair, in a condominium these matters have to be resolved through agreement. Endless meetings take place as every would-be soap box orator declaims his views on, say, whether first floor residents should pay the same for the lift as do those living on the eighth floor. Those living on the lower floors may not feel too pressing a need to repair a leaking roof, similarly those on the higher floors may not be overly concerned by malodorous drains. The hard-up widow may strongly resist proposals to repaint the lobby. If the block employs a *portiere* the salary and conditions will have to be agreed. All these decisions are taken at condominium meetings, which are frequently prolonged and acrimonious. The residents' voting rights are decided by the size and location of their flats. Often an *ammistratore* is appointed from among the residents to carry out the day-to-day administration of the block and is usually paid a small allowance.

The disadvantage of a condominium is apparent: there is tremendous scope for falling out with your neighbours. A new owner's part in the condominium is spelled out in a document which goes with the flat. This must be read and understood before you agree to buy. It is sensible to pay attention to what is going on at the condominium meetings. If you do not attend them, or appoint a proxy, decisions, usually involving money, will be taken without you having any say.

If your intention is to find a property yourself and buy it privately getting in touch with local estate agents is advisable. At least the prices they are asking will give some guidelines, however rough and ready, to local market values. They can also be extremely useful, particularly if the time you can spend house-hunting is limited. The sudden foreign demand for rural housing in central Italy caught local estate agents, whose bread and butter were urban flats, completely by surprise. Many estate agents in Tuscany and Umbria are foreigners, either working for themselves or attached to local firms. If you are relatively young, and unqualified, there are few ways of making a living once you have set up home in rural Italy. Those who do not want to teach English or do technical translations, have found the property business a lucrative alternative.

Inevitably, the trade is not run along formal lines. Few agents have offices and usually appointments are made in village piazzas and bars. One estate agent who has invested in an office makes the point that if you are unhappy at least you can come along and smash the windows. This is reassuring up to a point, although the agent is, perhaps, being optimistic if he thinks severely dissatisified clients will limit themselves only to breaking windows.

The one point that potential buyers should never forget is that you pay estate agents simply to find houses for sale. Nothing else. An estate agent is not a source of impartial advice. One British couple, who had been shown a large house in Tuscany by one agent, were very surprised to be shown exactly the same house by another. This time the price was nearly 50 per cent more and they were assured planning permission for a swimming pool would be no problem, which was not the case.

If you want to know about planning restrictions, speak to a lawyer or a *geometra*, or go to the local comune. When you decide to buy, all contracts and researches should be carried out by a lawyer. It is astonishing how many people buy houses in Italy without taking the kind of precautions which would be second nature in Britain. It is also astonishing how much money can be lost if a blunder is made. The author knows of two people who paid about £30,000 each for houses they had not seen, merely discussed over the telephone. They were lucky and got reasonable houses. But anyone who does this and discovers that their dream villa in Tuscany turns out to be a shack in Florence's *zona industriale* is unlikely to receive great sympathy.

Estate agents in Italy, of whatever nationality, are no more dishonest than estate agents anywhere else in the world. But, similarly, the Italian breed enjoys no higher public confidence than does our own and there have been scandals. Ostensibly, most estate agents claim a percentage commission, payable when the purchaser signs the initial contract (*compromesso*) to buy the house or the completion document (*il rogito*). The commission may be included in the price or be added on - this must be ascertained immediately. Usually it is between 2 and 3 per cent. It is important to inquire closely into this before even looking at an estate agent's properties.

Sometimes, however, the price has been loaded and the vendor and agent have come to their own agreement on splitting the proceeds. To crack down on cowboys a new law was introduced in February 1989. All legal estate agents in Italy must be registered. This means they will have a document from the local comune which will use words such as *mediatore per il ramo beni immobiliari urbani e rustici* to describe their occupation. All estate agents must be Italian or from EEC countries, be educated to *diploma* level (in this case, the equivalent of City and Guilds qualifications), have had two years apprenticeship in an agency and have passed an exam. Illegal estate agents face fines of between L1 million to L4 million and after five offences may be sent to jail. How this law will work in practice is far from clear. Many estate agents are now registered, but I have met none who have undergone the apprenticeship or exam. Italian agents, late-comers to the *case rustiche* market, refer to the law to establish their bona fides as opposed to foreigners who have set up as freelancers. But for all its good intentions, the law is not going to stop wide-boys, whether apparently legitimate or not. However, for those who are reassured by such things a list of all registered estate agents in Italy can be obtained from:

> Federazione Italiana Agenti Immobiliari Professionali,
> Via G. Pisanelli 25,
> 00196 Roma.
> Tel: (06) 39 11 959

BRITISH ESTATE AGENTS

Compared with Spain or France few British estate agents sell property in Italy. In fact, about ten. Some have been around for some years, others appear and vanish very quickly. Many British newcomers are made up of former agents in the British market, who have found the present conditions unrewarding. Others had employment in the City. All are worth getting in touch with. They produce particulars, which are usually not very detailed but often include a photograph or sketch. Through looking at these, a good idea will emerge of what the top end prices for houses are likely to be.

The majority of these agents concentrate on the lucrative pickings in Tuscany and Umbria. It is because of their influence that little pockets of British residents develop, such as around Umbertide and Città di Castello in Umbria. Don't be deceived, incidently, by talk of "branch offices" here and there which these estate agents like to go in for. Most have been set up by individuals, or couples, who find themselves in Italy. They know the area they live in and have collected a list of local property which is for sale. Most have friends in England who run the advertising and answer inquiries. It is rare that they even have an office. Of course, these are not important considerations so long as you remember what you are paying (and handsomely) the estate agents for: to find you a suitable house for sale - *and that is all*. A list of British-based estate agents appears on pp.172 - 75.

For those wanting private sales, Italian property is regularly advertised in *The Sunday Times, The Observer, The Independent* and, naturally, in the local Italian newspapers.

Many of the British-based companies offer to arrange viewing tours, including flights and hotels. These are not recommended. The more agencies you visit and talk to the better your understanding of local conditions is likely to become. It would be a major mistake to commit yourself to one estate agent before you have even arrived in Italy.

Generally, the arrangement for payment is commission on sale. Do not get involved in paying research fees of any kind unless you know exactly what you want and, better still, know the person you want to employ.

5 Buying Property

Once you have found the house of your dreams and agreed a price for it with the vendor, the next step is to begin the process of buying it. Before doing anything, however, it is vital to obtain advice from a local lawyer (*avvocato*). Many Italians, particularly in country areas or when buying flats, do not use lawyers. This is because all property transactions involve a public notary (*notaio*) and follow well defined procedures. These advantages, coupled with Italians intuitively knowing the ropes, means legal advice can be dispensed with. The same is not true for foreigners. Making a mess of buying a house is always expensive: hiring a lawyer reduces the dangers.

The conveyancing process works like this. The *notaio* undertakes certain superficial searches, such as checking that the vendor actually owns the land, that the land is correctly registered and no illegal extensions or buildings have been erected. Although the choice of *notaio* is the purchaser's, he is an impartial public official who represents neither party's exclusive interests.

A number of researches are immediately necessary. To begin with, it may be a good idea for a *geometra* to go over the property, assess its structure and estimate how much any intended works are likely to cost. The financial standing of the vendor will need to be checked. If a loan is secured against the property, then it can be repossessed from the new owner after sale by the creditors. *Notaios* should uncover this sort of thing easily enough, but it cannot hurt to have your own lawyer also making inquiries. Of course, an unwitting buyer can challenge this sort of thing in the Italian courts, but not without expense and anxiety. No money, incidently, should be paid to the vendor while simply looking over the property.

COMPROMESSO

Once a decision has been made to go ahead with the purchase, the buyer and vendor draw up a preliminary sales contract (*contratto preliminare*), generally referred to as the *compromesso*, which outlines the conditions under which the property will change ownership. In this crucial document, which is a private agreement but can be enforced by the courts, the vendor undertakes to sell the property and the purchaser to buy it. The *compromesso* will state the price of the property and the date by which the transferral of ownership must take place. In addition, the purchaser will pay a deposit to the vendor, preferably through the *notaio*, of about 25 to 30 per cent of the price, although as little as 10 per cent may be accepted.

It is important that this deposit is described as a *caparra confirmatoria*, subject to article 1385 of the Civil Code. If the vendor were to refuse to proceed with the agreed sale, the purchaser has the legal right to demand from the vendor a sum equivalent to twice the deposit. Similarly, if the purchaser does not complete the contract within the time specified the vendor keeps the deposit. This happened to a British family who found that they were unable to sell their home in East Anglia during the property slump in the summer of 1989. They could not go ahead with the sale and so lost their L20 million.

Compromessi will often have many other clauses, particularly if Italian lawyers are involved because they delight in re-writing them. Often the penalties for non-completion will be made even more severe - some *compromessi* have insisted that the vendor return three times the sum of the deposit if he reneges on the sale. Other conditions are more prosaic. There may be clauses about water supply, rights of access, even details such as cleaning out the stables or removing an abandoned tractor. The property will be identified by urban or rural land registry references (of which more later) and will include a map. When the properties are vacant, vendors will often let the purchaser move in after the *compromesso* has been signed and paid. If for some reason a deposit of more than 50 per cent is insisted on, then the transferral of ownership, and occupation, should take place immediately.

Most *compromessi* are signed in a lawyer's office after vendor and buyer have gone over the document and understood it. It can be dealt with by proxies, or even signed and sent through the post. It depends on the conditions, but if you want a farmer to clear out his stables before completion it is no bad thing to emphasise this verbally to his face.

ROGITO AND TAXES

Before the *compromesso* time limit expires, and you must ensure that it is sufficiently generous to move funds from Britain to Italy, the public act of sale (*il rogito*) is signed in the *notaio's* offices with both purchaser and vendor, or their proxies, present. (A proxy would typically be a local lawyer. The necessary authority - *procura* - can be obtained through an Italian consulate, but this is often so tardy many prefer to use lawyers in Britain who can cope with Italian law, a more expensive but quicker way of doing things.) The *notaio* checks that all the conditions of the *compromesso* have been fulfilled and registers the property in the name of the new owner. The balance of the purchase price and other dues are now paid. The public act of sale will typically take place about six weeks after the *compromesso* has been signed, although this can vary widely. Generally, no interest is charged on the balance payable. This too must be confirmed at *compromesso* stage.

As with stamp duty in Britain, in Italy purchasers of property have to pay registration tax (*imposta di registro*). The taxes differ according to the designation in the land office of the house, which can be either rural (*casa rurale*) or urban (*casa urbana*). A rural house is an agricultural dwelling which is interdependent with its land. A designated urban house, however, does not have to be within an urban area. It can stand alone in the middle of the countryside and have a certain amount of land attached. Buyers of *case urbane* pay 8 per cent in registration tax, and those of *case rurale* pay 15 per cent. (Much lower rates exist for special cases, such as smallholders in depressed rural areas, first-time local buyers in some comunes and for historic buildings.) In addition, the buyer pays land registry fees (*imposte ipotecarie e catastali*) making the total approximately 10 per cent for a *casa urbana* and 17 per cent for a *casa rurale*.

At this point the question arises, on what figure are you going to pay tax. In Italy, as elsewhere on the continent (including sleepy Belgium), it is widespread practice to underdeclare the price paid for a property and thus avoid paying what is generally regarded as an excessive tax. The vendor, of course, is even more keen to see a lower figure on the *rogito* because he faces capital gains tax (*imposta comunale sull'incremento di valore degli immobili - INVIM*). The kind of bargaining that would not be out of place in a Middle Eastern souk often evolves in the *notaio*'s office as the vendor encourages you to agree to an absurdly low sum for the property's declared price (which saves him capital gains tax). Here the role of your legal or financial adviser is essential. The advice is likely to be to follow local ways. But do not be greedy, and do not forget that however widespread the practice may be it is nonetheless blatant fraud to the Italian state. It is always difficult for foreigners to understand that in Italy rules are obeyed, sometimes approximately, but only in extreme cases ignored altogether. An excessively low declared price would be a provocation to the authorities, and if they decide to carry out exemplary punishment for some reason the chances are they will choose a foreigner.

The amount declared on the *rogito* varies in different areas. In Umbria the figures are about 45 to 60 per cent of the price paid; in Tuscany closer to 60 to 80 per cent; whereas in Rome or Milan they are closer to 90 per cent, because the value of property is widely known. In the South the figures could be anything.

You can insist on declaring the exact price you have paid for the property on the *rogito*. Unless the vendor is prepared to renege on the deal, and pay back your deposit twice over, there is nothing he can do about it. You will, of course, be considered completely mad.

When deciding the sum on the *rogito*, bear in mind that it is not in your interest for it to be too low. The *rogito* is your most credible document so far as insuring the property is concerned - although the real price will have been stated on the *compromesso*.

It is also important when removing capital out of Italy, which still has exchange controls. If there is a possibility of you selling the property in the near future and leaving Italy bear the following in mind: if you pay £100,000 for a house, but only declare £60,000 on the *rogito* and then sell the house for £120,000 in six month's time you are left in a quandary. If you declare £120,000 as the official re-sale price you will be liable for substantial capital gains tax. If you declare, say, £65,000 you may well experience difficulty removing the remaining cash out of the country. Sound local advice is terribly important.

The Italian government is well aware that under-declaration of property prices is practised by everyone (which is why the tax is so high). To attempt to counteract this tax evasion, a law (Decree 131/86) was introduced in 1986 allowing the authorities to revise official property values (recorded in the local land offices) and bring them into line with their market worth. The law allows the value to be determined by the assumed statutory income (*reddito catastale*) of the property. For buildings this is the assumed annual rent and for land it is agricultural revenue. These figures are multiplied by 60 and this total is what the authorities consider to be the true value of the property. It is recorded in the land registry and adjusted in line with inflation. The law is now being applied throughout Italy and is bringing about a degree of uniformity.

But the practice of under-declaration is unlikely to cease. The new system is bound to undervalue property, particularly rural property. Foreigners, and Italians seeking a villa in the country, are prepared to pay far higher prices for attractive farm houses than simply an estimation of their value as working holdings. Astonishingly, land that is to be built on is specifically excluded from the system although it is likely to change hands at the highest prices of all. In its brief life the law has been immensely controversial, even challenged in the Italian Constitutional court. But it is clearly here to stay. Property subject to Italian inheritance tax (*imposta sulle successioni e donazioni*) and capital gains tax (*INVIM*) is assessed in the same way.

Once the *rogito* has been signed, it is also time for the buyer to sign the cheques. In addition to the actual property price, the buyer will have to pay the taxes, *notaio*'s charges (approximately 2 per cent of the declared value), estate agent's

commission if not included in the purchasing price and
personal lawyer's fees.

The table below gives an idea of the total charges likely to be
incurred when buying a rural property costing - without in this
case estate agent's fees being included - £30,000.

Actual purchase price	£30,000
Personal lawyer's fees (2%)	£600
Transfer taxes (17%) on declared value (say £20,000) of the property	£3,400
Notaio's charges (2% of £20,000)	£400
Estate agent's commission (3% of £30,000)	£900
TOTAL	**£35,300**

PROBLEMS

As soon as all the money has been handed over it is not
unknown for the *notaio*'s offices to become truly festive. Bottles
of *spumante* are produced and toasts drunk. In out of the way
rural areas, these festivities can mark the beginning of the
newcomers' acceptance in the local community. Buyers who
leave everything in the hands of proxies rather miss out.

But inevitably, for a few buyers, the joy of owning a home in
Italy can quickly go sour. In the majority of cases this is because
fundamental precautions which buyers would not dream of
omitting when buying property in Britain are foolishly skipped
in Italy. Thus it is that people have bought their long-desired
Italian retreat only to discover in the first few weeks that they
have paid way over the odds for the pleasure. There is, of
course, no sure way round this possibility, but buyers should
always discuss the property's price with the vendor, *and always*

meet him. It is essential to find out whether the asking price is the same sum that the vendor expects to receive. If it is not, then the estate agent is loading the price and needs to do some explaining. The practice of inflating the price, yet still asking for a generous commission, is not unknown.

Property which is owned by estate agencies should be scrutinised carefully. Prices should be compared with other houses in the area. Speak to neighbours, disinterested professionals (lawyers, *geometri*), and other foreigners in the area. If you do buy a property owned by an estate agent, it is against the law for a commission to be added to the purchase price.

As buying property in Italy involves two stages, it is not unknown for speculators to buy up *compromessi* on desirable homes. An agent buys a *compromesso* at 30 per cent of the house's value and then has, say, six months to find a foreign buyer prepared to pay a higher price than would be obtained locally. The scene in the *notaio's* office in these instances is far from festive. The vendor will realise, at this stage, that he has undersold his property, while the buyer will know that were it not for the middle man the price would be far more attractive. Of course, the speculator runs the risk of finding no one who wants the property and therefore, under the conditions of the *compromesso*, either having to buy it himself or losing his deposit. Large houses have changed hands in this way and it is an obvious way in which estate agents can make substantial sums of money, as opposed to simply commissions.

Another major problem is the possibility of buying property which has been secured against loans or mortgages. These are usually quickly identified in the searches - but trust your lawyer here, rather than relying solely on the *notaio*. Incidentally, do not be afraid of buying a house - with advice - which is mortgaged. The price may take into account the inconvenience of taking over the loan. Given high Italian interest rates (unless the property is a smallholding or some other special), the mortgage is usually best paid off in one lump sum.

Rights of a coltivatore diretto

But the greatest danger facing foreign purchasers of rural property concerns the rights of adjacent smallholders to buy your house *at the price stated on the rogito*. The law here varies from region to region, although the aim is the same. In central Italy, in particular, agriculture has been in crisis for many years. To help smallholders, *coltivatori diretti*, build up sizeable farms they have the first right to buy rural property (this applies only to property registered as a *casa rurale*) which actually borders their land. In Italian this is called *il diritto di prelazione* - the right of pre-emption. If a *coltivatore diretto* has not waived this right when a rural house is sold, he can exercise it up to two years after the date of the sale. The right of pre-emption applies only to property which actually abuts that of the smallholder.

In one instance, this law threatens to bring complete ruin to a family who bought a substantial rural home in Umbria. They did not use lawyers, but instead relied on the inadequate advice of an estate agent. The house was bought for L120 million, although on the *rogito* the declared value was only L40 million. In the first six months the family gutted and re-roofed the house, put in new kitchens, several bathrooms and a swimming pool. The cost of this work came to around L300 million and, as is customary, much of the work was done without any proper receipts or payments of VAT. It was at this point that the neighbour, a *coltivatore diretto*, exercised his right to buy the property at the price paid on the *rogito*, plus compensation for improvements which could be accounted for with official receipts.

In other words, the neighbour stands to buy a luxury villa at a knock-down price well under £100,000. For the moment, the foreign family remain in possession. The matter may, expensively, work its way through the Italian courts, where it could remain for many years. Alternatively, it has been hinted that for L20 million the smallholder would be prepared to drop his claim. Neither option is cause for satisfaction. An additional point here is that the price on the *rogito* was plain greedy. The absurdly low declared price, only 33 per cent of the price paid, must have been an additional enticement to the smallholder.

From the above it is clear that before buying a rural property (which means land and buildings in Italy) it is essential to get the *coltivatori diretti*, who can also be a tenant, to waive their purchasing rights. Your lawyer's advice here will be crucial. One way may be to send a registered letter to the *coltivatori diretti* asking whether they are interested in purchasing the property for the declared price. If there is no reply within - in some areas - 60 days, then their purchasing rights expire. A more simple solution is to get them to sign the *compromesso*, thereby accepting the sale of the property to someone else. The price on the *compromesso* and the *rogito* must be the same. This method only works if there is co-operation - as would be a blanket statement from the *coltivatore diretto* that he had no interest in buying the property.

If it is clear that the *coltivatori diretti* will not voluntarily waive their pre-emption rights, you should think again about buying the property. You are unlikely to enjoy harmonious relations with such neighbours. However, determined purchasers have been known to draw up complicated rental-purchase agreements with the vendor. This involves transfering the freehold of the farmhouse straight away, but then renting the land from the vendor until the smallholders' pre-emption rights expire after two years. It sounds very complicated.

Another rather inadequate solution is to state in the *compromesso* that the vendor must ensure that the neighbouring *coltivatori diretti* will not exercise their right of pre-emption. This does not make much sense because it is the buyer, not the vendor, who is going to suffer most if, 18 months after the sale, the *coltivatore diretto* begins to feel acquisitive.

A far superior solution, followed by many purchasers, has been to get the vendor to re-register the house as a *casa urbana*. This involves employing a *geometra* to draw up the internal plans of the house (not required for *case rurali*) and re-registering the property at the land office. The procedure costs about £200. *Case urbane*, and the land around them, are not affected by rights of pre-emption and can be bought without this risk.

In most cases, of course, the local *coltivatori diretti* are reasonable, friendly people who have no intention of creating difficulties. But it should be as clear as day to any purchaser, given the risks, that the advice of a lawyer familiar with local ways is essential.

To be designated a *coltivatore diretto* at least 70 per cent of your income must come from the land, worked by yourself or with limited assistance (in other words, you are not a large landowner). However, revenues from *agriturismo* (bed and breakfast, riding schools, fishing and so forth) also count as agricultural income. This means foreigners in the holiday letting business are beginning to see benefits in becoming *coltivatori diretti* - for example, cheap loans and government grants.

One British lady, who is a *coltivatrice diretta* producing wine near San Gimignano, used her pre-emption rights to guarantee her privacy. She was horrified when a young couple from Chelsea tried to buy a fallen down cottage overlooking her home. The couple planned to build terraces and a swimming pool in a position of unwelcome proximity. The lady contacted the vendors telling them she intended to exercise her purchasing rights and the couple from Chelsea had to seek their dream home elsewhere.

Blatant fraud in the Italian property business is very rare. This is particularly the case in central Italy, which is law abiding. When Edward McMillan-Scott, a Conservative MEP, undertook a study of "transfrontier property transactions" for the European Parliament, he found little evidence of crooked practice in Italy. Commenting on his report, which was published in March 1989, Mr McMillan-Scott said:

> "The basic picture is that 90 per cent of problems occur in Spain. Partly this is because Spain is where most British people buy property, but also because the country is riddled with corruption, bad practice and a joke legal system. Also the kind of people who buy in Spain seem to be in a slightly different category. University professors buy property in Tuscany to retire, whereas miners from Doncaster use their redundancy to go and buy a place on the Costa Blanca. It is as simple as that. The economic resources of people buying in Italy tend to be stronger and so is their ability to work out how to do it. This is also true of Greece and, to a lesser extent, Portugal."

After seeking out British residents in Umbria, the main complaint Mr McMillan-Scott encountered was that buyers often paid over the odds for their homes. This seems a minor matter compared with the horror stories related from the Costas in his report. As in Spain, there is a considerable amount of illegal housing in Italy, particularly in the South. Periodically, there is a general amnesty and owners of illegal housing (*edilizia abusiva*) pay relatively small fines to make their properties legal. In general, foreigners should not get involved in illegal housing. There are many inconveniences: no local authority water, electricity or telephones can be connected and your right of residence, and therefore much else, may be affected. The dismal speculative developments along the coasts are frequently illegal. Foreigners should avoid them - they are, in any case, absurdly over-priced. It is also far from reassuring that *mafia* and *camorra* money is behind much of the building trade in the South.

MONEY

Most of the British who buy homes in Italy do so outright. Those who intend to live there permanently have generally sold off their homes in Britain. Others are spending savings, or legacies or some other cash. Few want to borrow. There are a number of reasons for this. Times have changed since the Medici and the other Renaissance businessmen who developed modern banking and double entry book-keeping. For all its triumphs in manufacturing, Italy has appallingly inefficient financial institutions. The controlling interest in all the major banks is held by the state. There is no real competition between them and there has been very little incentive to provide consumers with an adequate service. Anyone who has had to waste the best part of an hour changing a traveller's cheque will know this well.

Building societies are a British phenomenon and the banks that provide mortgages do so on a very restrictive basis. Few are prepared to offer more than 50 per cent of the property's value and the pay-back time is commonly 10 years. After initially making contact with a bank, delays checking the would-be mortgagee's income, value of the property and so forth waste about three months - by which time the vendor might have lost interest.

In the past, this state of affairs provided the high-earning British communities in Milan and elsewhere with hours of fruitless moaning. This is now changing. In May 1989 Abbey National Mutui Spa opened offices in Milan and offered 85 per cent mortgages repayable within 20 years. The main aim was to attract Italian mortgagees, but the service, which is quite new to Italy, is proving popular with expatriates and those wanting to buy holiday homes. Applications are handled in the same way as in England. The home loans can total up to three times the applicant's income, taking into account other financial commitments. The property is assessed by an approved surveyor (*geometra*) and it is valued. (In the case of a freelance *geometra* being employed - for property outside the Milan area - a sworn valuation will be required.) The whole process can take place in a few days - an alacrity completely alien to customary financial practice in Italy. At time of writing (September 1989) the rate of interest is 14.4 per cent.

The main disadvantage for anyone who is still earning in Britain is that the loan is vulnerable to currency fluctuations. In the past two years lira has been more stable than sterling. If sterling collapses for any reason, you lose. And you could lose rather a lot for as long as sterling remains outside the European Monetary System. It is against Italian law for a mortgage in Italy to be issued in a foreign currency; and it is unusual British banking practice for a loan on a foreign domestic to be issued in Britain. For those who intend to live and work in Italy, British-style mortgages may be a welcome alternative to paying grasping old signoras an excessive amount of rent. In time, Abbey National will issue mortgages in ECUs which will limit the effect of currency fluctuations within Europe.

Another potential source for home loans are special financial institutions catering for niche markets. Some companies, such as Benetton for example, offer a limited degree of financial services. The best deal so far encountered has been 80 per cent mortgages re-payable after 15 years.

But why haven't mortgages taken off in Italy? Is it because Italians might simply walk off with all the money? Apparently not. Richard Allman, the manager of Abbey National Mutui Spa, said: "So long as you can carry out the proper vetting procedures then the Italian market is probably a better bet than the UK, in having more ability to repay. They tend to take the onus of repaying the mortgage more seriously, quite frankly, than do the British. It is more of an honour and a commitment. That is not to say there are no bad debts, there are, but our vetting procedure knocks most of them out anyway."

Mortgages of 100 per cent are not likely to gain ground, however, given the atrophied state of the Italian courts. Repossession of a property would take about three to four years. Mr Allman has no doubt that the property market is going to expand: "Italy is a growing market that is in the same position that Spain was in four or five years ago."

BUYING OFFSHORE

For those buying modest properties in Italy there is little to be gained in setting up an offshore trust. The legal fees involved are likely to outweigh the benefits and paying the taxes would probably work out cheaper. But for the wealthy or those who wish to make substantial investments in Italian property there are considerable advantages. The most convenient tax havens, or offshore centres as they prefer to be known, are likely to be the Channel Islands or the Isle of Man, although Switzerland or Luxembourg, in this instance, would do just as well.

A hypothetical example will illustrate how the process works. An individual sets up an offshore trust, or has one set up on his behalf, settling say £250,000 on himself, his wife and two children. Sometimes even grandchildren will be included because it is wise to make the trust as wide as possible initially, avoiding the complexities involved in adding individuals later on. The trustees would typically include a professional trustee, a member of one of the legal practices which have sprung up in the offshore world, and a relation or two, but not any of the trust's beneficiaries. The professional trustee, who will run the trust, must be dependable.

The trust then forms a limited company with, say, £5,000. It then lends the company the £250,000 (free of interest, unsecured and repayable on demand) and the company buys the villa. It does nothing else. It certainly does not trade, nor make itself liable to tax. As a company does not die, there is no liability involving death duties. Any transfer of ownership would also not be taxed, as you sell to the new owner simply the shares in the company. One drawback is that every ten years domestic property in Italy owned by foreign companies is liable to tax, but it is small compared with the transfer taxes mentioned above.

The advantages of this arrangement apply only if you cease to be resident in England. If you were still resident, the British tax authorities would tax the offshore money in the same way as it taxes everything else. However, if you were resident in Italy, and all the financial arrangements were made before you moved there, your offspring would pay nothing.

Nowhere more so does that rather lame phrase "seek professional advice" apply than in any dealings with the offshore world.

6 Renovations

The following is quoted, more or less at random, from particulars of a house - charmingly renamed *Mulino Tranquillo* - sent to potential buyers by the estate agents, Property 1992.

"An old, three-floored mill in a valley near the medieval village of Montisi [Tuscany]. ... The ground floor is made up of old animal stalls and the cellars. The two spaces entered by the arched doorway are brick-vaulted. Outside at ground level can be seen the tops of the two brick-vaulted tunnels which run beneath the house, through which water once used to flow. The two rooms to the south as well as having beam and *cotto* [terracotta] brick floors (a rarity for stable areas). The first floor consists of the old kitchen with its original fireplace and five further rooms, two of which are reached via separate entrances from outside. From the kitchen an internal staircase leads up to the second floor, which consists of two further rooms. The floors and ceilings are in good shape and are made of original materials. The outbuildings include the old pigsties, the old bread oven and a small stone barn. The house is not attached to the mains electricity, but the lines of supply are close (about 200 metres away). As for the water, the mains supply is nearby and the cost of hooking in would be minimal. There is also a well which gathers the water run-off from the roof. What is more, the fact that the property is set next to a stream would suggest that there is a good likelihood of being able to sink an artesian well without difficulty. A feature of note is that the traces of the huge old stone *vasca*, which acted as the

water reservoir above the house still remain. As such, one
is assured of permission to build a swimming pool
because the comune cannot refuse you permission to
restore the mill to its former glory. The property has its
own tree-lined driveway. The house comes with
approximately two hectares of land, though the owner is
flexible. Price: £60,000."

One does not need to be a master of the art of reading between
the lines to realise that acquiring a property such as the above is
likely to involve greater expense than simply the purchase
price. Estimates vary, but those in the know reckon that to
renovate a delapidated country house will cost between one
and two times the initial price paid. This is why an initial
estimate from a *geometra* on the likely costs is so important.
Building work in Italy, usually of a far higher standard than in
Britain, does not come cheap. Michael Goodhall, a British
architect who lives and works near San Gimignano, estimates
that to re-do a house from scratch costs between L800,000 and
L1,000,000 per square metre of usable floor space. To refurbish a
house which is basically sound, and does not need a new roof,
the price can come down to L500,000 a square metre. A labourer
will charge about £10 an hour and a skilled one would be cheap
at £12.50. Much money can be saved if you are accomplished at
DIY, an unfamiliar art in Italy. To get a precise estimate of the
costs is always difficult. Once work begins invariably more
problems present themselves. The only sure advice is never to
underestimate. It is probably a case of coming up with a figure
and then adding on a bit more, for bad luck.

If you do find a property which would be ideal, but needs a
lot of work, balance out whether the effort involved is going to
be worthwhile. Those who have bought a holiday home may
find little relaxation in three weeks of unremitting DIY and
hassles with builders. Getting things done from Britain involves
expense and the risk that work will not be satisfactory. A British
property developer in Umbria found it impossible to get his
garden wall built in the right place during his absences. There
are small companies, often run by British people living in the
area, which undertake to supervise building work. Only when
you return to Italy will you discover whether this was a good

idea or not. Those who intend to live permanently in Italy are in the best position to do up a house according to their wishes. But speak to any foreigner and you will hear heroic tales of endurance through the winter cold as building work grinds on at a snail's pace - or stops altogether when there are frosts. People have grown old waiting for things like water, electricity or a telephone to be connected. The record, I think, must be held by a British family near Colle di Val d'Elsa, in Tuscany, who have waited 15 years for electricity. The pilons carrying the current were ready to be erected when an absentee landlord accused the village of stealing one of his bullocks. To encourage immediate reparation, he refused to let the electricity board on his land. The matter is now in the hands of the courts. In the meantime, the children have grown up and gone elsewhere to discover the twentieth century.

It is thought by some that the better bargains in Italian rural property are to be found in partially refurbished housing, where major works are unnecessary. This is something only individual purchasers can weigh up successfully. But if the house has a roof, doors and windows and is not flooded, at least you can live in it from day one.

Opinions are divided about Italian builders. Most foreigners highly rate the quality of their work, but others find them slightly unimaginative. One home owner had great difficulty in getting his roofers to fit a glass tile. Used to heavy, flat terracotta tiles of a design unchanged for centuries, the roofers said such things did not exist. The owner then made his own, using heavy industrial glass, cut to shape, and some glass adhesive. There was great reluctance to fit this tile and, after it was done, dire warnings that hail would smash the glass to bits. Four years later it is still firmly in place.

Some Italian builders have successfully talked themselves out of the lucrative business with foreigners by demanding excessive prices. The British, ungifted in the arts of negotiation, have looked elsewhere. One retired City accountant living near Lucca was so distressed by the Italian builders' estimate that he brought over a team from Britain. This worked very well. The British builders enjoyed the change and the owner got what he wanted. Another person tried the same thing with less success. The British builders arrived laden with tins of peeled tomatoes, spaghetti hoops and similar. But after three months their provisions were exhausted and they had got bored. Leaving the job half-done, they demanded payment and threatened to report the home owner to the local comune for using black labour unless he paid up. For some unaccountable reason, the owner succumbed to this self-defeating blackmail.

For all the undisciplined sprawl around Italy's cities, planning controls are very strict - provided they are not ignored altogether. This is more of a southern habit, than the practice in central Italy's efficient Communist-run local authorities. Here planning controls are strict and there is a perceptible will to protect the rural beauty of the environment. To anyone used to the ways of the South, the probity of these Umbrian and Tuscan comunes is staggering. One example will suffice. The Communist council of Castiglione del Lago, on the western side of Lake Trasimeno, was given a grant of about £50,000 to help develop tourist facilities. After long deliberation, during which the burghers rejected several plans including a proposal to develop a luxury hotel, it was decided that the money could not be spent and it was returned. Such an outcome would be unheard of south of Naples - indeed, the story itself would be disbelieved.

In planning matters the distinction between a rural house and an urban house becomes important. A rural building, whether the farm house or the pigsties, is deemed to be interdependent with the land and has no value apart from it. In the local land office, the *catasto*, the property will be registered with a land plan showing only the outline of the buildings. There will be no details of what the internal rooms are used for. An urban house is registered with a full draughtsman's plan of the house, or flat, with measurements of elevations, window sizes, internal walls and doorways. There are advantages and disadvantages in both designations.

Let's say you buy a ruinous traditional farmhouse with outbuildings which is designated a *casa rurale*. You want to convert the old stabling arrangements on the ground flour into liveable rooms, such as kitchens or dining rooms. The outbuildings you want to turn into holiday apartments. Undeniably, your aim is to change the buildings from agricultural to residential use. It is unlikely, the house remaining a *casa rurale*, that you would get planning permission for this. The answer is to change the house into a *casa urbana*.

A couple of points before proceeding. If this is your intention you would be wise to find out what the local authority policy on developments of this nature is before buying the house. Secondly, planning permisssion is granted in rural areas of Italy for a variety of reasons. In one area near Siena, for example, it is said that planning permission for swimming pools is virtually impossible to obtain since the mayor opened a holiday complex with bathing facilities.

Changing a property's designation takes some time and a degree of expense. The request is usually made by a *geometra*. The planning authority can vary. Sometimes it is simply the comune, but it can be a collection of comunes - *intercomunale* or *comprensorio* - which make decisions on what in England would resemble the "county plan". One factor which will influence the authority's decision is whether it is thought appropriate to reduce the agricultural land - the number of *case rurali* - in your particular area. A detailed ground plan of the house will have to be submitted, which then forms part of the land registry records. If permission is granted the house will have to correspond to the health and building regulations which, as a rural house, it may have escaped in the past. The process costs about £200.

Once the house is redesignated a *casa urbana*, you can put forward your planning applications, again to the local comune. Detailed *geometra*'s drawings of the proposed improvements have to be supplied as well as a plan of the buildings in their present state (basically a copy of the plans supplied to obtain redesignation). Sometimes even photographs are required. In many parts of Tuscany and Umbria permission is rarely given for the house to become larger or its external appearance to change radically. Materials which are not typical cannot be used nor can large modern windows be blasted through the stone walls. There are fines for those who transgress these rules. One British resident near Umbertide, in Umbria, was astonished to discover he had broken the planning regulations by fitting arched as opposed to rectangular windows in his secluded cottage. The fine was £60, which was considerably less than removing all the offending windows.

Once the plans are submitted to the comune, the relevant committee will in time come to a decision. Usually this is within three months, but nine-month waits are far from unknown. One reason for further delay is if the house is of particular artistic or historical importance, in which case the application also has to be referred to the *Ministero dei beni culturali ed ambientali*, in Rome. Once 90 days have passed with no reply from the ministry, the "silence is assent" regulation applies and the comune can process the application in the usual way. If it is in favour of the proposed changes the comune will issue permission, *concessione edilizio*, allowing three years for the work to be completed, renewable if necessary.

Unlike the redesignation of the property, planning permission involves taxes which vary greatly in different areas from L4,000 a square metre to L15,000. Even more curious is that some comunes levy the tax only on the part of the building which is actually going to be altered, whereas others levy it on the whole building. In the latter instance, if you own a mansion and simply want to build a downstairs lavatory the taxes involved may make you reconsider introducing this facility, however welcome it may be. There is also a percentage tax on the estimated costs of the work. Most comunes will allow these taxes to be paid in instalments, without interest. Non-residents may have to provide some guarantee that they will pay the taxes, usually from the Italian bank where they have an account.

Going through the process of redesignation of a property and obtaining planning permission can be quite wearisome and, for some people, not worth the effort. There are sound reasons for retaining the rural house designation. You may want to grow vines, raise livestock, set up a riding school or attempt to cultivate some government grants for *agriturismo*. So long as the changes to the property are not that great, redesignation would not be necessary in any case. For example, if you simply want to make the ground floor, stables area of your house liveable, there is no reason not to do so, provided no structural work or extensive plumbing is involved. A dream jacuzzi fitted into the cow stall might be difficult to explain. The important point is that such changes do not prevent the property conforming to its description in the land registry. If this happens, it can become unsaleable, with the *notaio* simply refusing to proceed with the sale as soon as he spots the discrepancy. As ever in Italy, local advice on these matters is essential.

There is, no doubt, a line of logic in the Italian planning regulations, but it is not immediately obvious. One healthy development is that some comunes are now applying a law which allows property owners to make internal alterations to their homes without paying taxes. But still the work has to be authorised, and there are penalties if you just go ahead. Given the variations, offering some guidance of the costs of planning consent is clearly impossible. One owner of an urban house near Umbertide, in Umbria, paid L130,000 for permission to turn an open portico into an enclosed kitchen. In other parts of the country he might have had to pay twice that, or perhaps only half.

7 Residence and Working

To judge from the amount of bureaucracy involved, Italian officialdom appears to be deeply suspicious of foreigners and likes to keep a close eye on them, even if they are Euro-cousins. It must be added, though, that foreigners are not treated much differently to the locals. In Britain there are many who think identity cards are only a goose-step away from all manner of repressions. In Italy, it is against the law for citizens to be without their *Carta d'Identità*, which everyone is issued with. There are also an infinite number of certificates for this and that, which regulate their lives. Italy is a liberal democracy, of course, but there are one or two traces in its government apparatus of less happy regimes.

Foreigners visiting Italy should register with the police 48 hours after arrival. But those staying in hotels, *pensioni* and organised camping sites are automatically registered by the management. Anyone planning a longer stay has to apply to the local *Carabinieri* for a *permesso di soggiorno*. This is given readily enough provided the applicant has sufficient means of support and has some reason for being in the country (students, work, setting up home etc). Interestingly, it can also be given for *motivi famigliari*, which usually means marriage with an Italian but can be living together (*convivenza*), which is a *stato di famiglia* under Italian law.

While people are house hunting, or organising works to make their home livable, the *permesso* will be granted for three months, usually for "tourism". Three photographs are required and the application, as always with the Italian bureaucracy, has to be made on infuriating *carta bollata* (legally stamped documents, which can be bought from tobacconists and some government offices). The whole procedure takes up the best part of a morning and costs about L3,000. Thereafter, the *permesso* can be renewed annually, again on *carta bollata* and with three new photographs. Once you have bought your home, where you intend to live permanently, you must register your family with the local comune. You will need to show passports, birth certificates (also for offspring) and, if the property is jointly owned and you are a married couple, a marriage certificate as well. These should all be translated, with if possible a British Consulate's stamp emblazoned all over them (thus avoiding the expense and hassle of having to use official translators). Your civil status (*stato civile*), and that of your family, is now well and truly incorporated within the embrace of the Italian bureaucracy.

The first requirement is a *certificato di residenza*, which after the *soggiorno* is the most important document that permanent residents are going to need. Its first use will be in transporting furniture and other possessions to Italy. A copy of the *residenza* and a list of the property will be needed by the freight company. These will be presented to the Italian customs when crossing the border. Without the *residenza* the goods would be liable to duty and IVA (Italian VAT). In theory, the transportation of personal effects must take place within six months of having taken up residence in Italy. Any subsequent removals are taxable. In practice, this does not happen and there are those who have moved even large amounts of furniture long after the first six months have passed. Unlike Spain, there are no rules about how long you have owned the property, nor do you have to give any undertaking that you will not sell it. After 1992, with harmonisation, these restrictions should be scrapped in any case. The bulk of the paperwork will be handled by the specialist removal company. For those who do not intend to live permanently in Italy, a copy of the house purchase agreement can be accepted in lieu of a *residenza*.

Residenza has another, long-term importance. So far as the British tax authorities are concerned, it is your most convincing declaration that you are no longer resident or domiciled in the UK. This becomes particularly important on death. If the tax authorities regard someone as having been domiciled in Britain, in spite of having lived for years abroad, an estate will be liable to inheritance tax. It is important to clear this question up with your legal or financial adviser as soon as you make the move.

Residenza is the source of many other *certificati*. With it driving licences can be obtained, bank accounts opened (not always a requirement for this), health care claimed and children sent to local schools. It can be used to obtain a *certificato di stato civile* (civil status), which many employers and universities insist on. This gives details about your family, marital status, religion and children. There is also a *certificato di cittadinanza* (citizenship), which may at times be required especially in cases of mixed nationality marriages, and a *certificato di famiglia*. There is even such a thing as a *certificato d'essistenza* (a life certificate), required to claim pensions.

It cannot be stressed too strongly that in Italy regulations differ from comune to comune, for no particular reason. If someone is in an officious mood all manner of *certificati* may be required. Those who own holiday homes and have no intention of living permanently in Italy escape the worst of this. Indeed, one couple who spend prolonged periods of the year at their flat in Campania, have never troubled themselves with even obtaining a *permesso di soggiorno*. This is in spite of - or possibly because of - having the local *maresciallo* of the *Carabinieri* as their next-door neighbour.

The worse thing to do is half fill out a *soggiorno* and then not go through with it because you don't want to waste the time. This results in a fine. So too does forgetting to renew it every year.

MAKING A LIVING

According to the leaflet of the British Embassy at Rome " ... there is much unemployment in Italy. It therefore follows that anyone who does not speak fluent Italian and has no special skills has little prospect of finding a job here ... Anyone who, despite these warnings, decides to try their luck here should bring sufficient money to support themselves for several weeks and to enable them to buy a return ticket in the (all too likely) event that the search for work proves unsuccessful. People with no visible means of support are likely to be picked up by the police, charged with vagrancy and escorted to the nearest border."

This leaflet has a faintly familiar ring and the author seems to recall coming across it ten years ago when he was a student. These days it gives a misleading impression. While it is true that the prospects of manual labour in Italy are not too bright, for the vaguely professional there are countless opportunities. Teaching English and doing technical translations are an established means of earning a crust virtually anywhere in Italy. There are also a lot of secretarial jobs and those connected with the holiday trade, such as in hotels. In Milan there are between 10 and 15,000 British people, the majority under 40, who work in every form of business: fashion, advertising, TV, design, banking, law, broking and so forth.

In rural Italy there are estate agents and those in the villa letting business who do very well. Indeed, for many people who move to these areas the importance of making the investment pay is keenly felt. This is quite possible. One recent arrival in Umbria bought a detached, large farmhouse, with spectacular views over a valley, for £80,000. The house was in good condition and needed little work. Two holiday apartments were created and for an additional £12,000 a small swimming pool was built. This is a great attraction for holiday lets. The income from the lets will be easily £20,000 a year. There are few houses in Britain costing approximately £100,000 from which one could draw such an income. Of course, the capital value of the property is going up all the time and the family live there throughout the year. EEC nationals have the right to take up or seek work in Italy. Those who are looking for work, but are not resident in Italy, are given a tourist's *permesso di soggiorno* valid for three months. When a job is found, the *permesso* will be adjusted, and the police must be notified of the name and address of the employer immediately. A *libretto di lavoro* is then obtained from the local *municipio*, which is the equivalent of a work permit and record. The *libretto* is kept by the employer or, during periods of unemployment, by the equivalent of the Job Centre, *Ufficio di Collocamento*. It used to be the case that sacking anyone in Italy was virtually impossible, so liberal are the labour laws. However, the mass lay-offs at Fiat in the 1980s changed matters somewhat. Nonetheless, it remains the case that employers must prove dishonesty or serious misconduct and pay-offs are normally made (these extend even quite low down the workforce to secretaries and clerks). The result of this legislation is that it is quite difficult to get a permanent, legally recognised job. Most employers prefer to employ "black labour", paying cash out without bothering to inform the authorities. The black economy, or *economia sommersa* as it prefers to be known, accounts for a good deal of Italy's present prosperity. Many Italians have more than one job, particularly those employed in lowly state occupations. A few years ago, when Rome airport insisted that all employees turn up on one day, it was found there simply was not enough office space to accommodate them all. Early retirement was introduced to reduce the number of state employees and there were cases where 25-year-old women were retiring, to live off their pensions. Italy has the largest bureaucracy in Europe outside the eastern Bloc, and jobs within it are sometimes little more than a form of "dole". Again, it must be stressed, that if you do find yourself working in the black economy you must make sure that you take sensible advice.

For the self-employed there are various forms of trading company. Unlimited partnership (*società in nome collettivo*), the most simple form of business arrangement, are those in which all partners are liable for all the debts and obligations of the partnership. It is set up by at least two people in the presence of a *notaio pubblico* who drafts the partnership agreement (*atto costitutivo*). The documentation has to be filed at the local *tribunale commerciale*, which then authorises it. Registration tax at the rate of 1 per cent on all capital and assets introduced must be paid. The partnership name must include the name of at least one of the partners and be followed by the initials *SNC* in all publicity.

Slightly more complicated are limited partnerships (*società in accomandita semplice*), which has general and limited partners, the general partners being jointly liable for the partnership's obligations and the only ones who can manage the partnership or have their names included in the partnership name. Limited partners are liable only to the extent of their investment. The partnership name must include the name of at least one of the partners and be followed by the initials *SAS*.

Limited liability companies (*società a responsabilità limitata*) must have a minimum capital of L20 million. Finally, there are corporations (*società per azioni - SPA*) which have a minimum capitalisation of L200 million. Liability of a shareholder is limited to the amount of shares.

8 Arranging Your Finances

The overwhelming majority of foreign residents in Italy maintain the banking arrangements they have already made in their own country of origin. There are several sound reasons for this. First among them is that Italian banks are inefficient. The most simple process can take an absurd amount of time as forms are filled in on clapped out typewriters. (These can, of course, be quicker than computers. The record time wasted in a bank by the author was due to the system going down). One example perhaps illustrates the general banking milieu in Italy. A branch of a major bank in Rome changed an American Express traveller's cheque with no problem. A couple of days later it changed another, but charged L5,000 for the transaction. Why? After all, the banks make a good enough turn on the exchange rates. The cashier was surprised. Taking the customer's word that there were usually no charges on traveller's cheque transactions, the L5,000 was simply dropped. Such a friendly and accommodating solution to a problem is rare and welcome. But it does make you wonder whether your savings would not be safer under the mattress.

More important, is that Italy still has exchange controls. In Britain it has been forgotten how inconvenient and disruptive controls used to be. Of course, with 1992, capital should be able, in theory, to pass freely over the national frontiers. Until then exchange controls remain in force. At the time of writing (September 1989), foreign residents in Italy can remove L5 million every time they leave Italy, but only L1m of it can be in cash (the remainder would be travellers' cheques, banker's draft etc). As in the past in Britain, this allowance extends to children.

Another important consideration is that if you transfer all your assets to Italy they are far more open to the attentions of the Italian tax men. This is not prudent. A limited amount of money will have to be transfered to Italy and a bank account set up. Most people do this at the time they are actually buying their home. The necessary money is transfered from banks in Britain, through an Italian bank in London to a branch near where the foreigner plans to live. Homes are generally purchased with a banker's draft, *assegno circolare*. Thereafter the attractions of having a bank account in Italy become obvious. Additional large sums can be fed into it from Britain, cheques can be used and standing orders set up to pay electricity, water and gas bills.

But even those who have lived in Italy many years find it makes sense to keep their British accounts and credit cards going. Those who are retired can have their pensions paid into their British banks in the normal way and cash Eurocheques, acceptable at all the major Italian banks, when funds are needed. People working in Italy, paid in lira, will find more need of an Italian bank account. Because of exchange controls, savings cannot simply be passed on to the bank in Britain. To do this, you must physically take the money with you, by a banker's draft for example, when you leave the country.

The most attractive investments foreigners are likely to make in Italy will be in businesses they themselves have set up or in real property. You must know what you are doing before having a punt on the Milan stock exchange, where insider dealing is the norm and most of the big deals don't take place in the market at all. Italian banks have high interest bearing accounts and often the rate is negotiable with each individual customer. It will depend on the amount of money deposited. Interest is paid free of tax and it is up to the customer to declare it.

If money is left on deposit in Britain it is essential to inform the bank if you are no longer resident, otherwise it will be taxed. Many find it attractive to transfer their accounts to the Channel Islands, where all the high street banks have offices.

From the above it will be clear that most expatriates will require a financial adviser. Choosing one is always difficult and, yet again, it is a question of personal recommendation. It is particularly important to get things right if you are dealing with tax havens. The Channel Islands or the Isle of Man have obvious advantages for English speakers. Under the Financial Services Act 1988, it is illegal for an investment adviser or private portfolio manager to practise in Great Britain or the Channel Islands without being a member of the Financial Intermediaries, Managers and Brokers Regulatory Association (FIMBRA) or one of the other watchdog organisations responsible to the Securities and Investments Board. Firms which are members of FIMBRA must indicate this on their stationery and advertising. The air: of the Financial Services Act, and FIMBRA, was to provide a greater degree of protection for customers against firms which go bust or are fraudulent.

There is always some degree of risk in an investment. The slow and steady end of the business, involving blue chip companies, aims to provide a regular and reliable return for an investment. Where there are hopes for larger, short-term profits the risks increase proportionately. Neither FIMBRA, nor the other organisations, provide compensation if you have simply been unlucky. However, if the investment firm you are using cannot for some reason *meet its obligations to you* there is a compensation scheme, run by the Securities and Investments Board, from which you can make a claim. The maximum you can receive is £48,000. The scheme does not have unlimited funds and if claims in a year exceed £100 million the payments to claimants will be scaled down. FIMBRA also runs an independent adjudication scheme operated by the "Investment Referee" which can require a FIMBRA member to compensate a client who has lost money, up to a maximum of £50,000. There is no cost involved for complainants (although legal advice may be required).

The aim of the Financial Services Act was to regulate what is, of necessity, a risk-taking industry and reassure potential clients. Up to a point it succeeds. But the important point is to choose the right adviser at the start. The sanctions of the Act do not apply to independent subsidiaries of British companies operating in Italy.

A list of members can be obtained from: FIMBRA, Hertsmere House, Marsh Wall, London E14 9RW. Tel: (01) 538 8860 or (01) 895 1229.

Details of stockbrokers, futures dealers, life insurance companies and unit trust managers, which are governed by similar schemes, can be obtained from: Securities and Investments Board (SIB), 3 Royal Exchange Buildings, London EC3V 3NL. Central register enquiries: (01) 929 3652.

Any company which is not a member of FIMBRA, or the other organisations responsible to the SIB, should be approached with circumspection.

TAXATION

Nobody likes paying taxes, but Italians seem to dislike paying them more than others. For those used to dealing with our beloved Inland Revenue, or who have been visited by the VAT inspectors, it comes as some surprise to learn that many Italians pay no income tax at all. It has been estimated that in 1984 unpaid taxes would have accounted for the government's entire annual debt. Tax evasion takes place on a huge scale and there is daily evidence of it. Cash transactions are still the order of the day, even for large amounts of money. Things have changed slightly since 1970, when less than 30 per cent of entire government revenue came from income tax - indirect and transaction taxes and government monopolies made up the rest. In spite of the efforts of reformers, taxation has not been used as an instrument of social policy. No beaming Denis Healey has announced - with any likelihood of success - that he would "Soak the rich". For the small-scale entrepreneurs who are the backbone of the country's revival this state of affairs is very agreeable. For many others too - except the very poor, whose condition might be improved if the responsibilities of the state were wider.

But most Italians are quite happy to frustrate the state, and even the poor have precious little faith in its beneficial influence. Past experience has taught them better. Fiddling of VAT, *Imposta sul Valore Aggiunto*, became so blatant that now there are severe laws concerning receipts. The *Guardia di Finanza* can arrest you and impose swingeing fines if you leave a restaurant without a proper *ricevuta fiscale* (fiscal receipt). The monopolies of salt and tobacco - sources of finance which existed in pre-revolutionary France - are also avoided. In the Seventies, a large part of the economy of Naples depended on cigarette smuggling. The authorities did nothing, fearing a crack-down would drive the *camorra*, and those who depended on the trade, into even worse criminal activities. On the Naples sea front you used to see the blue motorboats of the smugglers moored directly opposite the powerboats of the *Guardia di Finanza*, but nothing was done apart from a chase or two, which led to the smugglers being stuck in the sea with no fuel (more effective and expensive than a fine). These days the trade has fallen off and the *camorra* is into more lucrative cocaine dealing (the *mafia* handles heroin). The South, one must never forget, is a different country. In Naples there is even a market in contraband petrol, which is very expensive in Italy.

It is a peculiarity of Italian law that citizens are responsible for declaring themselves for tax with the local fiscal authorities (*Intendenza di Finanza*). Until you do so it is unlikely that the tax men are going to pursue you. So why bother to pay any tax at all? The point here, as in so much of Italian life, is not to transgress the bounds of reasonable behaviour. For those who have never encountered Italian law it probably seems a bit of a joke. But there is seldom much laughing to be had when in the end, for no clear reason, it finally decides to pounce. If underhand dealing is discovered, life can become very uncomfortable indeed. British people who have set up businesses and not paid a lira in tax, and who drive around in British registered diesel cars (avoiding high taxes on diesel vehicles), are riding for a fall. Even more so if they are successful, exciting the envy of one's neighbours.

The advice is find a *commercialista*, the equivalent of an accountant, who is personally recommended, and pay the taxes which he advises. Not paying anything is stupid, and in a way an insult to the intelligence of the local authorities. This, they do not like.

The main form of direct taxation is personal income tax or *Imposta sul Reddito delle Persone Fisiche* (IRPEF). It applies, just like British income tax, to income received from whatever source: real property (thus, holiday lets), capital, employment, independent work etc. It is levied at the following rate:

Income	IRPEF rate
Up to L6,000,00	12%
L6 - L11,000,000	22%
L11 - 28,000,000	27%
L28 - L50,000,000	34%
L50 - L100,000,000	41%
L100 - L150,000,000	48%
L150 - L300,000,000	53%
L300 - L600,000,000	58%
Over L600,000,000	62%

For big earners the rate of income tax is considerably higher than in Britain. To counter tax evasion, the authorities have sweeping powers. Those suspected of fiddling will have certain assets assessed and a presumed income will, rather arbitrarily, be worked out. Signs of assets include second homes, yachts, hunting preserves, household staff etc. For example, the owner of a 12-metre yacht would be deemed to have an annual income of at least $6,300 per boat metre, or $75,600. A certain type of luxury car is evidence of income of at least $26,000 and so on. Those who live in a hovel and starve themselves perhaps to keep going a vintage Bentley could get a nasty shock. Tax on company income is called *Imposta sul Reddito delle Persone Giuridiche* (IRPEG).

In addition to the IRPEF income tax there is a local tax *Imposta Locale sui Redditi* (ILOR), which is raised on certain types of income received by individuals and companies. Although this tax goes to pay for services provided by the comune, provinces and regions, it is in fact levied and collected by national government in the same way as IRPEF. ILOR is levied on all income except that from subordinate employment, independent work, arts and professions, partnerships of any type and dividend income - which leaves, in fact, only the notional letting value of your property in most cases. (Income from business or agriculture is reduced by 50 per cent if this is the taxpayer's principal occupation.) ILOR is currently 16.2 per cent and works out generally less than British rates, or poll tax.

Inheritance tax in Italy, *Imposta sulle Successioni e Donazioni*, is not based on the value of the deceased's estate, but on the heirs and beneficiaries. In Italy, as in other western European countries, close relatives have an absolute right to a share of a deceased's estate. They cannot be cut off without a penny. Taxation law echoes this principle. If you are a direct relative then inheritance tax liability is at the lowest rate, cousins etc pay more and those outside the family pay the highest rates.

The following table gives an idea of how this works. Column A is applied to the total value of the taxable estate and Column B represents additional tax payable by heirs who are neither spouses nor direct descendants.

	A Rate on total inheritance	B Rates on amount of inheritance or legacy		
Taxable value		Brothers, sisters and direct relatives of spouse	Relatives in 3rd or 4th degree of spouse	Other persons
L1 -L2m	n/a	n/a	n/a	3%
L30 - L50m	3%	9%	12%	17%
L50 - L100m	5%	11%	15%	20%
L100 - L175m	8%	12%	17%	22%
L175m - L250m	11%	14%	19%	24%
etc until:				
L1,000m -	31%	19%	24%	29%

The temptation to leave everything to your spouse and draw up a memorandum of wishes for "other persons", whose tax liability increases sharply, must be great. Legacies to the Italian government (not common) and charities (*enti morali*) are exempt from tax and excluded from the total value of the estate.

Another important tax is on capital gains. *Imposta Locale sull'Incremento di Valore degli Immobili* (INVIM) is based on the increase in value of real property and is one of the most controversial taxes in Italy. Much of the anger surrounding it is because the assumed valuations for INVIM purposes are disputed. The tax is payable, in the case of individuals, either because ownership of the property has to transfer as a result of death or because it has been sold. In addition, companies owning domestic property must pay the tax every 10 years. This was to prevent them from avoiding the tax altogether by simply transfering share ownership.

Increase in value	Tax rate
Up to 20%	5%
20 to 50%	10%
50 to 100%	15%
100 to 150%	20%
150 to 200%	25%
Over 200%	30%

The above is a guide only. The way INVIM is assessed is complex and the subject of endless appeals and court cases.

Another tax foreign residents will encounter is registration tax on real property, which must be paid by a property purchaser within 20 days of the transaction.

Stamp tax is bound to be paid in any dealing with the Italian bureaucracy, and is an infuriating feature of it. All legal documents must be drafted on stamped paper, the dreaded *carta bollata*, which are bought from public offices or authorised dealers. Generally, the costs are around L5,000. *Carta bollata* must be used for even the most simple official actions. For example, a friend who applied for a lectureship at Rome University had to have the three or four lines of his MSc degree from the London School of Economics officially translated and typed up on *carta bollata*. The charge for this was about £50. In such circumstances, one must be prudent in making job applications.

9 Everyday Life

The British, as the Italian press occasionally points out referring to "Chiantishire" or Umbria, are thought to understand colonialism well. They like to feel at home and bring over one or two cherished institutions of their own. This may well be true to a modest extent, concerning small matters, like tea that is not stale or the occasional pot of Marmite. But so far as cricket is concerned, its extraordinary popularity in Italy owes little to the British now living there. In recent years it has taken off with Italians and there is even a league of clubs in Rome. The elegance and aesthetics of the game probably has something to do with it. New rules have been introduced, however, to restrict foreign players to only five in each team. Such is Italian competitiveness that good players were being enticed to join the teams from abroad. The rules are slightly different, and everyone gets a go at batting and bowling. It is all over in an afternoon, rather than drawn out over three days like the tests. In the past the game was not unknown to the Italians. Genoa soccer club, Italy's oldest, was called until recently "Genoa football and cricket club".

Even more recherché is the fox hunting to be had in Italy. La Società Romana della Caccia alla Volpe traces its origin back to 1836 when Lord Chesterfield set up home in Rome. His wife was suffering from bronchitis, and he needed some outdoor exercise during her convalescence. So reckless was the riding that when a tourist took a fall and died, the Pope attempted to ban the sport. He was unsuccessful, and the hunt still continues. Most of the riding is over the wild and beautiful countryside north of Rome. It still draws support from Roman nobility and enthusiasts, and has links with the Italian cavalry school at

Monte Libretti. Those interested in riding out should write to
the society at Via Appia 320, Capannelle, Roma.

Most of the British who live in Italy, particularly in the Italian
countryside, tend to live their own lives and blend into the local
scene. For those who wish to socialise and exchange gossip with
co-nationals there are many occasions to do so and there are even
one or two clubs. Florence, of course, has a large British
population, both resident and temporary, which focusses on the
British Institute and the library. In Umbria, it was a delight to
discover the English Speakers' Club. Its aims are stated in the
inaugural newsletter of June 1989:

> **A.** To give native speakers and others the chance to get
> together and talk English.
> **B.** To promote international goodwill - especially with the
> unification of the Common Market in 1992 in prospect.
> **C.** To help us all to pursue a variety of cultural activities."

The cultural activities are wide-ranging and include gardening
and videos of *Fawlty Towers* and *Sherlock Holmes*. The club's
formation excited hoots of joy from Dutch people living nearby
who immediately sent off L30,000 to join up.

Another aim of the club is to provide practical assistance.
Although one item in the newsletter reads ominously:

"An expert in Italian bureaucracy has agreed to write scripts
on coping with many aspects of Italian bureaucracy.
Unfortunately, he is bedridden at the moment, so he cannot come
to speak in person ... "

The club is run by Harry and Barbara Urquhart, San Lorenzo
di Rabatta 1M, 06070 Cenerate, Perugia. Tel: (075) 690693.

FAMILY LIFE

Apart from their appetite, both for food and the opposite sex, a
penchant for bursting into tears during sentimental songs and
driving habits which have changed little since the days of Ben
Hur, the caricature Italian is famous the world over for his
attachment to family. In Italy the family is everything. Its
importance is almost impossible to over state. In a land where

law and government can be weak, the family provides a reassuring security. With good family, and a powerful range of friends, many doors are open to you. University, jobs and a successful career are all easier to obtain if your family has clout. Troublesome distractions, such as military service, can be avoided. The poorer the family the more important it is. *Babbo stato*, the welfare "daddy state", is more apparent in Italy in the fine sounding laws framed by Parliament than in reality. If you are poor and have no powerful friends, you are likely to stay poor. Without family, and through it a *clientelismo* of friends, talent and ambition may not be enough. Of the three giants of Italian business, Giovanni Agnelli inherited his money ("I started at the top") and Raul Gardini married it. Carlo de Benedetti alone made it through sheer ability.

Yet there are those in Italy, particularly in the Catholic church, who feel that family life is in crisis. Certainly traditional values have had to change in the face of the extraordinary transformation of Italy in the past 40 years. It is true that today fewer young people are marrying, more are living together and there has been an increase in births out of wedlock. All these developments are far more pronounced in the North. However, so far as statistics are concerned, talk of family crisis seems exaggerated. Illegitimate births are, by northern European standards, relatively rare. Only 5 per cent of births in Italy are illegitimate, while in Britain the figure is 17.3 per cent (in Sweden it is 45 per cent). Divorce levels at around 3.8 per cent of marriages are well below the northern European average of around 30 per cent. The most extraordinary figure is Italy's enormous rate of abortion, which after a referendum is legal. Official figures estimate 457 abortions occur per 1,000 births in the North, compared with 262 per 1,000 in the South. These rates are far higher than anywhere else in western Europe and approach those current in Czechoslovakia and Hungary. It is all the more astonishing because all forms of contraception are easily available in Italy.

Like Britain, Italy's population is ageing and falling. The Istituto Centrale della Statistica estimates that by the 2020s the population will be down to around 48 million. This is regarded with alarm in Italy, where a high population is generally regarded as a good thing. These predictions are always unreliable. In Italy, as in Britain, the late 1980s have seen the birth rate increase again.

Marriage

Many British find themselves living in Italy because they have married an Italian. This is more common among women. According to the Foreign Office about two thirds of mixed nationality marriages involve British women marrying Italian men. Doubtless, most are blissfully happy with never a cross word exchanged. But the British Consulate at Naples is accustomed to pitiful scenes of young British women making their way to the office from Calabria or Sicily with a couple of black eyes and awful experiences of matrimony in the *Mezzogiorno*. They beg to be sent home. Romances which flourished on the disco floors of Birmingham can quickly cool in the deadeningly restrictive villages of Calabria or Sicily. Anyone contemplating such a union should think long and hard of what such a life is likely to entail. In remote villages it is often unusual for women to leave the house except when engaged on some domestic chore or for very special occasions. It is still widespread for mother-in-law to live at home and she will run the household, even distributing the husband's earnings on expenses such as children's clothes and food. Not surprisingly, many British women cannot cope and, after a time, head for the consulate and home. Others, who may have more resources of their own, flourish. One lady, an Oxford classicist, has been happily married to a comune clerk in an inaccessible southern village for many years.

The bureaucratic procedures involved in marrying an Italian are relatively painless, compared with the interminable frustrations that can be experienced in other matters. All foreigners must take a copy of their birth certificate to the comune in which they live. It must be translated into Italian. The Italian Consulate-General in London charges £3 for this service; British consulates in Italy do it for free. In addition a certificate of no impediment (nulla ost), called a *certificato di stato libero*, obtainable from British consulates in Italy, must also be shown. If you reside in Italy the comune will probably want to see your *certificato di residenza*. It is not a bad idea to have your passport as well as Italian authorities are fond of identity documents which have the bearer's photograph. Those who have been married, but whose former partner has died, may need to produce a translated copy of the death certificate. Those who have divorced may need a translation of the decree absolute. These requirements depend a little on the whim of the local official. All the above documents issued by the comune are valid only for three months so a prolonged period of indecisiveness, or delay, will result in everything having to be done all over again.

Italian spouses must obtain a *certificato di stato libero* from the comune, which will state whether they have always been single and, if married, when their partner died, their marriage was annulled or they were divorced. In the latter case, the marriage ceremony cannot take place in a Roman Catholic church. A divorced woman cannot remarry for nine months without special dispensation. This does not apply to widows.

The banns, or *pubblicazioni matrimoniali*, must be published at the *municipio* of the town where the marriage is contracted. They remain in place for eight days, including two consecutive Sundays. In religious ceremonies, the banns must be read out on two successive Sundays in church. If either partner is new to the area the banns will be published in their previous place of residence, even if it is abroad. They are also put up on the notice boards of some British consulates. Application for the banns to be published by the comune must be done in person by both parties. However, if this is not possible then a *procura*, power of attorney, can be obtained, for example from the Italian Consulate-General in London. Under-16s cannot marry without both father and mother agreeing.

Italian weddings are great fun, and slightly less reverential than British ones. Cameras flash away inside the church and, increasingly, videos record every moment. The photographers are in the habit of following the bride from the family home to the church. One wedding video had a preamble of about 45 minutes as the bridal car got stuck in a traffic jam. Viewing it all was hard going.

An important contractual arrangement is made before marriage. The spouses must decide whether they intend to hold their property together (*beni comuni*) or separately (*beni separati*).

This limits the claim each partner has on the other's property on death. Most young couples opt for *beni comuni*. With older couples, or with couples between whom there is a considerable difference in wealth, separation of property can exist. Thus an English woman who married her husband, a widower, when they were both in their forties maintained a separation of property arrangement. The husband died, leaving the widow to live in his flat which, because there were no children, will return to the husband's family after her death. Foreigners marrying Italians, and taking up residence in Italy, are exempt from customs duty and IVA on their wedding presents and trousseau, provided they are imported within six months of the marriage. The marriage certificate and residence certificate must be shown.

British subjects contemplating marriage to each other in Italy should think again. The bureaucratic complexities involved would in no way compensate for the pleasures, whatever they may be. It is far wiser to marry in Britain and, if required, have a service and celebration in Italy. All churches are prepared to do this.

Divorce

Divorce has been legal in Italy only since 1970, after a controversial referendum. At times it had been legal earlier. When Napoleon dominated the peninsula, divorce - which was part of his Civil Code - was one of his least popular measures among the Catholic hierarchy. On his fall, it was abolished for 150 years. Divorce is rare in Italy and it requires quite a lot of courage to go through with it. In a land where mortgages are not established, many family homes are initially bought by contributions from the families of the bride and groom, and there are generous wedding presents to furnish it. Among many people in Italy, therefore, divorce is a family disaster which affects more than just the couple. Clearly, there are couples who both have well paid jobs and can divorce relatively painlessly. But for most it would involve more agony than would be the case in Britain. For some it is not an option at all.

The grounds for divorce include mental and physical cruelty, adultery, desertion (*abbandono di tetto famigliare*, which is a criminal offence as well) and unsoundness of mind. The jurisdiction of the Italian divorce courts extends to anyone who either married in Italy or permanently lives there. The mother is generally awarded custody of the children and the husband has to provide maintenance. If, in Britain, you divorce your Italian spouse, whom you married in Italy, the divorce will not be recognised under Italian law. This has in the past made a bigamist out of at least one British citizen who re-married in Italy unaware of the law. To avoid this problem the British decree absolute must be recognised as valid by an Italian court , a procedure known as a *processo di delibazione*. For all its relative simplicity, lawyers have to be engaged to undertake this and there is no way of avoiding L2,000,000 in fees.

Custody of the children in marriages involving mixed nationalities which end in divorce is always a question fraught with grief. All the evidence seems to show that British courts tend to favour British subjects and vice versa in Italy. "Tug of love" cases, as they are known to journalists, are messy, expensive and seldom end happily. In the 1970s, a friend took the law into his own hands when the Italian ex-husband of his sister took the two children to Italy and refused to bring them back. Frustrated by the complexities and delays of the Italian judicial system, the brother, with a couple of friends, kidnapped the two children back. There was a dramatic race for the border as the *Carabinieri* gave chase, later related in breathless prose in the *Sunday People*. Needless to say, this is not recommended. It could easily have gone disastrously wrong, with the "kidnappers" even now behind bars in Italy.

WILLS

As soon as a death is brought to the attention of the Italian authorities all the deceased's funds and property are frozen. To avoid the painfully long delays this intervention inevitably involves there are occasional death-bed scenes which would not be out-of-place in an Eduardo de' Filippo farce. The stricken man or woman will often write a blank cheque which the family can then fill in after their death, withdrawing all the deceased's funds. One has yet to hear of an occasion involving a miraculous death-bed recovery in which a stricken father recovers only to discover that his son has pocketed all his cash. Doubtless, it has happened.

Under Italian law, as explained, long suffering wives and family cannot simply be cut off without a penny which, with certain limited exceptions, is the case in Britain today. Sad to say this does not mean that if your father decamps to Italy with his youthful mistress there still remains a chance of getting your hands on his cash. Under Italian law, the contents of a will made by a foreign citizen are governed by the laws of his own nationality. (This is also true in Spain, but not France.)

This law can present serious problems on the death of a British national, who either lives in Italy or owns property there. The difficulties arise because of the wide differences between Roman Law, which prevails in Italy and much of the continent (and Scotland), and Anglo-Saxon Common Law. In England (and Wales), Common Law developed the idea of a trust whereby property passes to executors who are the personal representatives of the person who has died. They then administer the assets for the beneficiaries. These may be the budgie, the Distressed Gentlefolk's Aid Association or, if they are lucky, the wife and family. Things become complicated, however, because Common Law trusts, with their notion of separate legal and beneficial ownership, do not exist in Italy. It can become very difficult to effect a British will.

Once someone has died, the first question Italian authorities are going to ask is who are the heirs to a particular property. This might be impossible to answer because the will directs the executors to sell, say, the villa in Tuscany and share the money out among four children, but exclude the widow who will continue to live in the house in England. Even more uncertain, to Italian eyes, are trustees who have been given discretion to select certain beneficiaries (ie if money has been left to "charity" the trustees must decide which one). The problem becomes more acute when the Italian revenue begins asking for death duties. Under Italian law, death duties - more correctly, succession duties - are assessed according to the degree of kinship of the surviving relatives. Widows and children pay the least and then increasingly heavy levies apply to distant relatives or total strangers. The intermediary stage of trustees, between testator and the heirs, can not only confuse the Italian authorities but can also involve additional succession duties. A professional trustee, for example your solicitor in England, who is not a next of kin is likely to incur the heaviest taxes if the estate transfers to his "ownership", as trusteeship would be considered under Italian law. When the trustee in turn passes the property on to the intended heir there is again, in Italian eyes, a change of ownership and another tax liability. If the trustee dies, or changes for some reason, while executing the property yet another stage of ownership is, theoretically, introduced.

Fortunately, such horrors seldom occur. The Italian legal system is well aware of these key differences between Roman and Common Law and, after the heirs have been duly terrified, a workable compromise is usually arrived at. However, anyone with property in Italy should ensure that a professionally drafted will is drawn up by a solicitor familiar with both legal systems. It is wise to avoid complicated trusts and always think of how the will is to be enforced in Italy. Making a wife or child the executor would limit the possibility of misunderstanding. Never forget, it is always expensive and can be *disastrous* to die intestate in Italy (or elsewhere).

In some cases, it may be worth considering two separate wills for property in Italy and England. Generally these would be two "English" wills. It could work thus: in a family of four, the husband would make one will for the Italian property and its contents and another relating to his cash, securities and property in Britain. So far as the Italian property is concerned all could be left to the wife, who should also be the executor of the will. Legacies to children, friends and charities would best be made from the British properties. Administration of the two wills can be kept separate and may mean the assets in one country need not be revealed to the revenue authorities in the other. In exceptional circumstances, it may be prudent to make an Italian will. In Italy, there are two common forms of will: the hand written holograph will, which does not have to be witnessed or registered with a notary, and the notarial *testamento pubblico*, which requires two independent witnesses and is registered. Only the latter variety is likely to be of interest to foreigners. It is essential if opting for a two will system, of whichever type, that professional advice is followed at all stages. Unhappy phraseology can result in one will cancelling the other, leading to the deceased being intestate or worse. Such a blunder would inevitably be expensive to resolve and time-consuming.

If the property has to pass on to a trustee, with all the tax consequences that that entails, a corporate trustee, which never dies, may be preferable. Property can be transferred to a trust before death or to a specifically constituted offshore company whose shares are held by trustees. Should the trustees wish in time to realise the property they may do so by selling the company, in that way avoiding taxable capital gains on the property itself. If they are to sell to other non-Italians the transaction is relatively easy; if they are to sell to Italian nationals it becomes more complicated, but a scheme is possible whereby with approval from the authorities an Italian company buys the shares and then the two companies merge into one. The costs of such an exercise must be warranted by the value of the property. Of course, after 1992 Italy's exchange controls should relax.

So far as taxes are concerned there exists between Britain and Italy a double tax treaty. This does not restrict one's liability to pay tax in one country or the other. The overseas assets of either a British or an Italian resident are taxable in the country of his residence and, in the case of land, also in the country where the property is situated. Property in Italy owned by a British citizen resident in the UK will first be liable in Italy, but a tax credit will be given against British Inheritance Tax payable on the same property. In the end one pays the higher of the two taxes, but not both. It is worth noting that UK Inland Revenue may not recognise the value for an Italian property which has been accepted by the Italian authorities. The Revenue may be curious why if £200,000 was transfered to buy an Italian villa ten years before, the villa's declared value on the owner's death is only, say, £120,000. Inspectors can be sent out from Britain.

A list of members of the Law Society with experience of Italian law appears on pp.179 - 80.

HEALTH

The Italians spend more - in total about £20 million a year - on their public health service than the British and get far worse value. The public hospitals are often disgracefully filthy and their organisation shambolic. There is no Florence Nightingale tradition of selfless nursing of the ill and, sometimes, judging by the dirt, no one has heard of Joseph Lister either. This is, after all, the country which managed to give the Pope - the Pope! - stale blood after he had been shot. In the South, the Third World rule applies: get to the airport, not the hospital. This is probably not a bad idea in the North either. In Naples' notorious Policlinico the wards are often filled with malingerers who use them as a place to sleep. In the morning they get dressed and go off to work. The country is over-staffed with doctors. So many used to enrol for medicine at the universities that posters had to be put up around campuses warning of medical unemployment. The training of doctors is often woefully inadequate and many graduate without having been present during operations or having dissected cadavers. Fortunately, many with medical degrees become health inspectors, epidemiologists and similar. Even in Umbria one hears horror stories - and there are too many of them to be simply stories - from those who have been admitted to public hospitals. There was a British nurse, who for some reason had to give herself all her injections. There have been times when there are no sheets, or food, or when there is food no cutlery. It is possibly unwise to expect too much. The National Health Service, for all its faults, is a unique organisation, the real value of which is only appreciated when compared with elsewhere.

Those who have got any money pay for private medical insurance and go to private hospitals, of which there are a great many, often run by the church. These are a complete contrast to the public hospitals, being clean and efficient. Most of the best doctors work in them. And Italy has very good doctors, in spite of the university system. The difficulty for foreigners is knowing where to find them. One can never be sure whether the distinguished surgeon is brilliant or simply owes his position to impeccable *clientelismo*. It is often safer not to bother to find out. If you need an operation have it back in Britain, where doctors have to undergo some of the most rigorous training that exists in medicine and the standard of competence is more uniform.

Most foreigners find it wise to have private medical insurance. The schemes run in Britain can be adjusted to provide international cover and are well worth obtaining.

One's health requirements are always unpredictable and so for all its shortcomings it is sensible to make arrangements with the public health service. Within the EC reciprocal arrangements exist, and British nationals should obtain an E111 from the DHSS. It is important to have access to general practice care, which is organised locally. Many of these GPs are excellent doctors. They have seen most illnesses, particularly the childhood ones, and can come to reliable judgements about the seriousness of the condition. Others may be less good but, as in Britain, they are the only source one has for prescription-only drugs.

EDUCATION

All Italian children and those of foreigners resident in Italy must go to school, which is compulsory from six to sixteen. Children who go through the Italian education system have all the advantages of bilingualism. This is far more than simply learning another language. It involves understanding a completely different and very rich culture. These are great advantages in life. There are differences, however. Italians are not, on the whole, great readers in childhood and their exposure to books can be inadequate. Reading for pleasure may be an interest which parents will have to encourage.

Unlike state education in Britain, particularly in the inner cities, Italian schools do not have a reputation for being a fertile ground for thuggery and deliberately acquired stupidity. Yob ethos has not put down firm roots in Italy, where to be thought *ignorante* is still a bad thing. However, as in some inner-city schools in Britain, drugs are a major problem. In parts of Naples mothers have organised themselves into vigilante groups to keep 14-year-old heroin dealers away from their children. The possible drawbacks in bringing up children in certain areas of Calabria, Sicily and Sardinia, where *mafia* culture prevails, have been discussed.

In the rural areas of central Italy, many British parents have put their children through local schools and, generally, have been pleased with the results. Italian education, helped along with exposure to books, seems to get a faster minded, more sensitive and intelligent end result than is likely to be the result in similar conditions in Britain. There is perhaps no real comparison with the British prep and public (independent) school system. This tends to be something you either admire or despise. Private schools in Italy do not have the same sort of tradition. Most exist for problem children, who for one reason or another have not managed to get on in the state schools. There is little of the class system in Italy which exists in British education. The prime minister's son and the local shopkeeper's go to the same school. Most British parents tend to think that the Italian education system is good enough up to university level. These are not rated as highly, and most try to get their children to go back to university in Britain. This is often successful.

Very few who have experienced Italian schooling have any regret about it. One girl, however, who had come to Tuscany when she was nine, bitterly missed friends she had made in England and never really got on with her Italian school friends. Bullying got so bad after the Heysel Stadium disgrace that the head teacher had to intercede and lecture the entire school. In desperation, the girl's parents sent her back to England to a boarding school, but after five years away she found she did not fit in there either and was utterly miserable. There is a flip side to this tale though. Her brother, who was only seven when the family came to live in Italy, has prospered at the same school, made lots of friends, is completely accepted and happy. The lesson here could be that it is better to move to Italy when your children are not too old and when you decide on a school try to stick with it. It may also be that as every child is different, no general advice applies.

Schooling, which is free, tends to start when children are about three at the *scuola materna* or the *asilo nido* (lit. "refuge nest", or kindergarten), which are not compulsory and are run by the local comune. The aim is to give mothers a rest or allow them to go back to work.

Between the ages of six and 11 is *scuola elementare*. School is school in Italy and the idea of creating a well rounded, mature child, while respected, is not thought part of the school's function. Typically lessons last only about four hours a day and then the children go home. There is seldom any attempt to provide painting, singing, dancing, drama, music and so on. These can be done elsewhere, in private clubs. Similarly sports are not a school function. Therefore, to provide a broadly based education along British lines, parents should expect to pay for additional tuition, music lessons for example, sports club fees and so on. Educational facilities are likely to be better close to larger towns, where you can expect a concentrated school population. Again central Italy is fortunate, being spared the industrial sprawl of the North and the excessive rurality of the South. It is also quite cosmopolitan, although almost exclusively European. International schools (see pp. 176 - 8) can be found in the main cities. Views vary as to whether they are a good choice or not. Some parents feel they isolate children from the communities they live in and accentuate cross-cultural differences. They are probably best for children who are only going to spend a limited period of time in Italy (such as diplomats' offspring).

In the state sector, at 11 exams are taken before moving on to the *scuola media*. The exams are not difficult, but they must be passed. *Scuola media* lasts until 14 and the curriculum is very broad. It is rare, however, for sciences to be taught at this stage and equipment and facilities are minimal. It would be unusual to find a school providing training in computers.

At 14 children take their most important school exam. The more academic will go on to *liceo classico* or *liceo scientifico*. Although the emphasis is either on humanities or sciences in the different schools, both are still taught and the rigid, and perhaps premature, specialisation at A-level is avoided. The less academic will go on to one of the more vocational *istituti tecnici*. There are various types: *ragioniere* (accountancy), *magistero* (teacher training), *peritotecnico* (surveyors), *agrario, industriale* and perhaps a few others. At 18 or 19, which is more usual, those at *liceo* take their *maturità*, which is similar to a baccalaureat in France. At the *istituti tecnici* the exam is a *diplomma*, which is a form of trade qualification, equivalent to City and Guilds, that helps to get a job.

Whichever qualification is obtained, everyone has the right to go to university - and has the right to study whichever subject strikes their fancy. A classicist can study quantum mechanics, for example. It is at this stage that many foreign parents living in Italy encourage their offspring to study abroad. This is particularly true of the British, who take university quite seriously and have a high opinion of their own. It is in any case thought healthy at 19 or so to travel, especially for those whose entire lives have been spent in Italy.

Although Italian universities have a mediocre reputation internationally, some are excellent. At Milan, the private Bocconi university has an extremely high reputation in business studies and economics. There is a special admission exam, and competition for the few places is fierce. Rome, too, has a private university called the Libera Università degli Studi Sociali, or LUISS. Again, it specialises in the money-making arts. Both universities are a mixture of London Business School and the LSE, with the Bocconi having the more illustrious reputation. Costs are several thousand pounds a year, although there are scholarships and some provisions for the hard-up.

It would wrong to give the impression that all Italian students aspire to go to these universities or that they occupy the pinnacle of academe. Italian state universities, like those in Britain, vary widely in quality. The Politecnico in Milan has one of the most distinguished engineering faculties in the world. Pavia is noted for medicine and Bologna, the oldest university in Europe, has a good all-round reputation. Pisa has its Scuola Normale, which requires exceptionally high grades to enter and has extremely high standards. Naples has the Orientale, the oldest oriental language school in Italy. When the British sent their first envoy to China in 1793, interpreters were engaged in Naples.

Teaching is even more remote and off-hand than at British universities, although with more excuse. Lectures are often over-crowded, sometimes to the point that you cannot get in. (Occasionally, they are embarrassingly empty.) Seminars and essays are not part of the curriculum, although a thesis, typed and elaborately bound, has to be completed. More so than in Britain, to get the best out of the experience students have to be self-motivated. One peculiarity is that exams can be delayed until the student chooses to take them. A recent visit to Pozzuoli, near Naples, involved joining a party to celebrate the award of a law degree. The proud graduate was all of 45. No degree can be completed in less than four years.

One of the added problems of education in Italy is that every male should, in theory, do military service. All kinds of practices are resorted to in order to get out of it. One friend even feigned insanity and was sent home after a couple of months by ambulance to Naples. It does not affect foreign nationals.

LAW AND ORDER

At a certain level lawlessness is rife throughout Italy. A commonly agreed distinction is made between sensible laws and silly ones, and little attention is paid to the latter. Italians think nothing of fiddling taxes, avoiding military service, not stopping at red lights if the road is clear, getting their hands on EC cash if someone is dumb enough to offer it and so on. But generally speaking while the letter of the law may not be adhered to, there is a social code of conduct. This means you should be considerate to neighbours, tolerate their peculiarities and not cause bother to anyone else. At its best, this sort of outlook produces a society which is free and uninhibited, avoiding the petty-minded "nerdishness" which British officialdom so often exhibits. At its worst, however, it means nothing is done when really nasty predators emerge, like the *mafia*.

It is strange, given the above, that Italy is inundated with police. There are more varieties - even *polizia veterinaria* (veterinary police) - than anywhere else in Europe, and all are responsible to different authorities.

The two main police forces in Italy with responsibility for law and order are the *Pubblica Sicurezza* and the *Carabinieri*. *Pubblica Sicurezza* is controlled by the ministry of the interior. The *Carabinieri* (literally, carbineers) are controlled by the ministry of defence and, in time of war, make up separate regiments in the Italian army. (In the rout at Caporetto during the First World War they achieved notoriety for the summary executions they meted out to retreating soldiers.) Both police forces are supposed to prevent crime and catch criminals, but there is no clear division between their responsibilities. Rather than work together it often seems that they are in competition with each other. One imaginative apologia for this surely unsatisfactory arrangement is that the two forces, by being responsible to separate ministries, cannot unite and enforce a police state on the nation. It is the *Carabinieri* who carry out sweeps - *rastrellamenti* - in the wilds of Calabria looking for kidnap victims, and who head the anti-*mafia* drives.

The *Carabinieri* have distinctive blue uniforms, white belts and pistol holsters, and double red stripes down sky blue trousers. They can occasionally be seen, ambling through the Galleria Umberto in Naples for example, wearing bicorn hats, white kid gloves, swords, cloaks and spurs.

The *Carabinieri* can stop drivers and demand on-the-spot fines. Periodically, they set up road blocks, often to catch *camorra* or terrorists, which must be approached with extreme caution. Like all the Italian police, and an alarming number of very unmartial bank security guards, they are festooned with arms. Tragic misunderstandings are not unknown.

Deemed to be incredibly thick, the *Carabinieri* have given rise to a genre of humour which is roughly equivalent to those side-splitting jokes the British like to tell about the Irish.

In addition to the above, there is another police force, the *Guardia di Finanzia*, which is equivalent to customs officers. They occasionally give chase to the smugglers operating out of Naples. Their responsibilities are not confined simply to watching the frontiers. If you leave a restaurant without a proper *ricevuta fiscale* (fiscal receipt), you can be stopped and fined. The *Guardia di Finanzia* are responsible to the ministry of finance and have yellow flashes on their uniform.

All towns will have *Vigili Urbani*, often recruiting specials during the summer at popular resorts. Municipal police can stop and fine drivers, usually for parking offences. They check up on matters affecting comune business: residence permits, planning infractions and so on.

It is best to have as little to do with Italian courts as possible. They have a dreadful reputation, which is thoroughly deserved. They possibly reflect their historical origin. Italy has an inquisitorial system of justice, not the adversarial system which was best evolved in England. Refined by Napoleon, the system was codified by Mussolini in 1931. Until 1989, an inquisitor (the *pretore*) handled criminal cases, which meant he investigated the suspect, questioned witnesses, determined guilt or innocence and decided the punishment. Without the involvement of anyone else, the judge had the power to sentence someone to prison for up to eight years. What is more he could easily be 25 years old, being part of a professional judiciary which is completely separate from the legal profession. Longer prison sentences would be decided by two or more judges.

In 1989 a new code of criminal procedure was approved which seeks to introduce the adversarial system. Prosecutor and defender can now call witnesses and examine them. Before, the lawyers had to pass memos to the judges, who asked the question, or not, depending on whether he thought it was worthwhile. One only needs to see the TV footage of the *mafia* super-trials in Palermo to realise that the Italian judicial system leaves a lot to be desired. Judge and accused often appear to be having a chat in the courtroom, with no evidence being presented or witnesses cross-examined. Under the new code, the *pretore* can no longer investigate, prosecute and find guilt solely by himself, and his powers of sentencing have been reduced to four years.

One would have thought that such a system would at least result in justice being swift. It is not. It is appallingly slow and incompetent. Two-thirds of Italy's prison population is waiting for a definitive verdict. At one point during the Seventies anti-terrorist legislation meant suspects could be held for 10 years and 8 months waiting for their case to be heard. Meanwhile, the matter was *sub judice* and the press could not comment on it. In 1983, 850 alleged *camorra* gangsters were arrested in Naples - 144 of them because they had the same name as wanted suspects. It took several weeks, in some cases months, before they were released. One suspect was Enzo Tortora, a TV games show host as loved as Bruce Forsyth in Britain. Tortora spent several months in prison before being charged and was only acquitted of all charges three and a half years later. As a celebrity, he has possibly suffered less than others, whose lives and livelihoods could be completely ruined by such an experience. There was no redress against the judiciary who were responsible for, if nothing else, such staggering incompetence. The concept of false imprisonment, let alone *habeas corpus,* is unknown in Italy.

THE MEDIA

Sad to say the Italian media, and television in particular, do not enjoy a very high reputation in the United Kingdom. Last year a British independent television company, attempting to see off some unwelcome European rivals, could think of no more wounding a counter-ploy than a series of press advertisements of a lady in underwear with the caption "Italian housewives do it on TV". Why the British television executives, given the appalling bad taste of their own products, imagined this arresting image would damage their rivals, and not fuel burgeoning Euro-enthusiasm especially among male viewers, beggars belief. The advertising campaign was further handicapped by the revelation that the lady in question was not Italian but a model from Slough.

However, members of Mrs Whitehouse's Broadcasters and Viewers Association who are considering a move to Italy need not necessarily reconsider their plans. Italian housewives don't "do it" on television, although they do strip off in front of the cameras in a show of truly delightful tackiness called *Colpo Grosso* (Big Hit). This is a programme which makes Cilla Black's *Blind Date* look like restrained good taste. Two contestants, a man and a woman, have to answer the kind of questions that won't get you an O-level these days and, if they are right, win millions of lira. The cash sums are displayed on a neon board in the shape of a woman dancer. If you have won one million lira her bodice lights up, two million and her bra lights up, three million and she is down to her suspenders etc. One of *Colpo Grosso's* hostesses then does a strip to the sum indicated. As each garment is removed there is thunderous applause from the studio audience. Intriguingly, the girls wear two pairs of knickers, only one of which is saucily discarded. Bosoms appear to be the show's anatomical preference. The contestants can win bonus points if they themselves strip off, which, looking rather awkward, they occasionally do. The show lasts an hour, although - such is its popularity - it is interrupted by lengthy commercial breaks.

To watch *Colpo Grosso* is to plumb the depths of Italian television, although it must be said there are an infinite number of dire quiz shows and dubbed soap operas which, if less prurient, are also far less funny. The best things on Italian television are the numerous films, which are far more recent than those shown on British television. On some channels the advertisement interruptions are so frequent they ruin the film. But then Italian ads are something of a televisual experience in themselves, particularly those involving housewives who burst into song, applauding washing powder or tinned tuna.

In common with everything else in Italy, the state-owned television stations are divided up among the ruling oligarchs. Politicians get their cronies into all the important jobs and few prosper in Italian state TV unless they have a *tessera*, or political party card. This system of political patronage is called *lottizzazione* and it is carried out quite without shame. Others might call it corruption, plain and simple, particularly British residents who have some naive notion that state broadcasting ought to be a public service. Usually when discussing these matters, Italian friends adopt a look of tolerant condescension, and ask "doesn't it happen in Britain?" I suppose the answer is, not to the same extent or so blatantly.

Of the three state-owned channels, the most popular is Rai 1, which is controlled by the Christian Democrats. Its 8pm *Telegiornale* programme reaches 12,000,000 viewers and is Italy's most important news source. Rai 2 is within the Socialist Party's sphere of influence and Rai 3, which shows more cultural programmes, is within the Communist Party's fiefdom.

The important independent television channels are Italia 1, Canale 5 and Rete 4. All are owned by Italy's emergent media billionaire, Silvio Berlusconi, who made his first fortune in Milanese property. Together they account for about 45 per cent of Italian viewing. Rete 4 is deemed more high-brow than the other two, but both are popular entertainment channels and none have a serious news service.

Italian radio does not stand any comparison with the BBC, which is unique in giving so much importance to this generally neglected medium. There is no *Today* programme in Italy. There is a sort of phone in during which a "distinguished journalist" philosophises about the state of the world. It seldom rises above the banal. Like television, the three state radio stations fall under the sway of political parties: Rai 1 is under the Socialist Party, Rai 2 Christian Democrat and Rai 3 (more cultural, with classical music and no advertisements) Communist Party. There are thousands of abysmal local radio stations, endlessly playing their one, scratched Duran Duran record and repeating the special offers advert at the local supermarket. Listen for long and you will go mad.

So far as Italian newspapers are concerned, the title with the most sales is the *Gazzetta dello Sport*. This fact speaks more for the country's total absorption with what news journalists refer to sneerily as "games" than with the quality of Italian newspapers, which is quite high. The *Gazzetta* is widely sold in the North and centre of the country, whose football teams it supports. The other big selling sports paper, *Corriere dello Sport* sells widely in Rome and the South. So popular are these papers that if you ask a Roman newsagent for a *Corriere* you are likely to receive the reply "*Dello Sport?*" The assumption is that you want to catch up on the latest football results rather than read the venerable *Corriere della Sera*, which is Italy's traditional equivalent to *The Times*.

Along with Fiat and a quarter of Italian industry quoted on the Milan stock exchange, *Corriere della Sera* belongs to the immensely powerful Agnelli clan. The newspaper, which began as Milan's evening newspaper and still has strong Milanese roots, has been the country's most influential newspaper almost since Unification. At the moment it supports Bettino Craxi, the tough chief of the Italian Socialist Party, probably more as a means of influencing factions in the far larger Christian Democrat Party than out of ideological sympathy. It is Italy's most authoritative newspaper and sells more than any other serious paper.

But the newspaper which has caused the most excitement in recent years, capturing the spirit of the Italy of the *sorpasso*, is *La Repubblica*. Founded in 1976 by the journalist Eugenio Scalfari, who used to edit *L'Espresso* news magazine, *La Repubblica* is the country's second selling newspaper (in fact, *Corriere della Sera* and *La Repubblica* regularly leap-frog each other in terms of sales). With *La Repubblica* rose the hopes of liberal Italy and the newspaper has long been an essential accessory for anyone with pretentions of cultural or political sophistication. When *The Independent* was launched in Britain, its closest role model was *La Repubblica*. Last year, a terrible blow was delivered to its prestige, and vaunted independence, when it was sold to Carlo de Benedetti, the chief of Olivetti and one of the most acquisitive of Italy's new generation of corporate sharks. The political line of *La Repubblica*, as with all De Benedetti's publications, is virulent opposition to Craxi and the Socialists (whom it originally supported). Craxi is regularly excoriated in the cartoons of Forattini, who depicts the charismatic Socialist leader and former prime minister as a reincarnated Mussolini.

Less influential, but an important and highly professional newspaper, is *La Stampa*, again owned by the Agnelli family. Based in Turin, its regional accent is pronounced and it defends the interests of the established Piedmontese industrialists. Sophisticated, with highly regarded cultural pages, *La Stampa* is politically conservative, tending to back the government of the day.

In spite of their importance within Italy, none of these newspapers match the professionalism of the four heavyweight British daily newspapers. A limited tradition of journalistic independence and concentration of ownership, worse even than that existing in Britain, ensure that fundamental questions concerning Italian society are not posed. The newspapers shamelessly grovel to the powerful: Giovanni Agnelli, head of Fiat, is the omniscient *L'Avvocato*; De Benedetti is *L'Ingeniere*, the engineer. Reports concerning their business activities are best treated with scepticism until corroborated in the *FT*. Cirino Pomicino, a Christian Democrat deputy and chairman of the important budget committee, has asked the question many have long wondered: "Some 70 per cent of the Italian press is either controlled or influenced indirectly by just two industrial groups, Agnelli and De Benedetti. Can you imagine what would happen if the two of them ever got together?"

News in the newspapers depends too greatly on agency copy and the staff reporters are given far too much space to analyse events not report them. Nonetheless, whatever their shortcomings at least the Italian newspapers avoid the appalling, insular navel watching of the British press. Most days the Italian newspapers give due prominence to the important world issues. The result is a far more balanced presentation of information than that given even in the quality British press (which not long ago gave more prominence to the discovery of glass in *six* tins of baked beans than the resignation of the Japanese prime minister). Not surprisingly, Italians are more clued up about the likely future direction of Europe than the British. For this the British press, in spite of its professionalism, has been woefully negligent. The exception, of course, is the *FT*, which is in a league of its own. Italy has a pink-papered financial newspaper, *Il Sole - 24 Ore*, but it does not compare with the *FT*.

There are a number of other influential newspapers in Italy. *L'Unita*, the organ of the Italian Communist Party, is the only big selling party-affiliated newspaper. After a prolonged dull spell, it is now enjoying something of a revival - an experience yet to be enjoyed by our own torpor-inducing *Morning Star*. *Il Manifesto* is a newspaper with far more influence than its pygmy circulation of 40,000 would suggest. It is a co-operative, independent newspaper with considerable influence on the Italian left. Scarce resources mean it is weak on news. Two other political newspapers are the right-wing *Il Giornale*, edited by the distinguished journalist Indro Montanelli, and the clergy-backed *L' Avvenire*.

There are also many provincial newspapers, such as the Socialist leaning *La Nazione* in Florence, the (Christian Democrat) *Il Mattino* in Naples, (Communist) *Il Messagero* in Rome and *Il Resto del Carlino*, in Bologna. One of the more interesting regional newspapers is *L'Ora*, a co-operative newspaper in Palermo. More than any other media organisation in Sicily it has been in the forefront of running anti-*mafia* stories.

There are countless magazines, many excellent and many dreadful. For the Italian equivalent of *Woman's Own* with a bit of *Tatler* thrown in try *Gente* (People) or *Oggi* (Today). *Epoca* is a popular magazine which addresses fairly serious issues. The numerous scandal sheets, which concentrate on sex and violence, enlighten another facet of Italian society. Try *Cronaca Vera* (Real News). Two big selling weekly news magazines are *Panorama* and *L'Espresso* (which is more important), both are owned by De Benedetti. Sadly, Italy does not have a satirical magazine like *Private Eye*. It is an unfortunate omission.

No English language newspaper is now printed in Italy. Not long ago two were produced in Rome. An extremely useful publication, even for those who do not live in Rome, is *Wanted in Rome*. It is an advertising sheet full of job offers, accommodation to let, cars for sale, furniture and so forth. It is distributed free all over Rome and copies can be obtained from its office at Via dei Delfini 17, Roma.

CARS

Those taking up permanent residence in Italy can import their cars without paying either customs duty or IVA (VAT) provided they have owned them, and used them outside Italy, for more than a year. There is a condition, however, that the car must be imported within six months of taking up residence. A *certificato di residenza* may have to be shown to the customs authorities, along with registration documents and proof that it is insured. Thereafter, the car can be used with its foreign number plates for a year, after which the car has to be registered in Italy and have Italian number plates (*targa*). Before this can happen the car will have to undergo the Italian equivalent of an MOT, called a *collaudo*, to see that it is roadworthy. A *collaudo* has to take place every 10 years. If you are not resident in Italy, you can bring your car in as many times as you like, but it must not remain in the country for more than a year without crossing the border.

Once the year is up, your car will have to be registered with the provincial authorities (*motorizzazione civile*). All car documents, and a residence certificate, will need to be taken to the relevant office. If change of ownership is involved, because you have bought an Italian car, a *notaio* will have to draw up a change of ownership document, rather as if it were land. Registration costs vary according to the size of the car (on which road tax, *passa di circolazione*, is levied), but even registering a small car costs about L200,000. You then obtain your Italian number plate and registration documents (*foglio di circolazione*). In Naples, and doubtless elsewhere, these may well be only temporary as there is a two-year wait for permanent car registration documents.

The whole business described above is time-consuming and special agencies now handle this sort of thing, for a fee, on clients' behalf. These are called *agenzie pratiche auto* and are well worth looking into. Remember that all cars will have to be re-registered if you move house into another province.

If you own an Italian registered car you ought, in theory, to have an Italian driving licence. This can be done by simply converting your own British driving licence. The Italian authorities, again at provincial level, will need a certificate stating that you have not been banned from driving for any offence. This can be obtained from any of the British consulates, provided you supply a copy of your birth certificate and a cheque for approximately L80,000. In practice, many British residents avoid doing this and obtain instead an international driving licence, which the police like because it has a photograph, or an EC licence. As always, it all depends on local circumstances. One Englishman in Naples still drives happily around with one of the old red cardboard driving licences.

Italian driving has an unfairly bad reputation. It is true that traffic lights are often regarded as purely decorative, that they undertake on the inside and commit countless other infractions. Nonetheless, Italian drivers have greater respect for the lives and limbs of others than the British, who are far more aggressive. They might go through red lights, but they don't run you down just because the lights are green. Anyone who has crossed the road from the Piazza Venezia to the Campidoglio in Rome will know what I mean. The cars shoot past you on either side, often with no slackening of speed. The experience requires some nerve, but whatever the manoeuvres of the cars your faith in getting over the road unhurt remains intact. Any attempt to do something similar at, say, Hyde Park

Corner, would simply result in you being run down - and with precious little sympathy.

PETS AND WILDLIFE

The British are well known for being quite inseparable from their pets. Few houses in central Italy owned by the British are without a hound taking a siesta panting and slobbering underneath the kitchen table. Cats and dogs can be brought into Italy with their owners, but there are regulations. The animal must have a certificate of health, translated into Italian, stating that it has been examined and found free of disease. The animal must also have been vaccinated against rabies not less than 20 days before it is brought into Italy and not more than 11 months. If this is not done it may be vaccinated at the border. Again a certificate of some sort needs to be shown. Some prefer to leave these matters to specialist firms.

Some local comunes insist that dogs are registered with the Unità Sanitaria Locale and are tattooed. It is in any case sensible that they are insured and have a means of identification. Accidents can be expensive. The owner of an unfortunate red setter, which wandered onto the Città di Castello to Perugia *superstrada* and was knocked down, had to pay £1,000 to compensate the car driver. As a result the owner pays dog insurance, which comes to L38,000 a year.

Rabies exists in Italy, and is currently (1989) supposed to be prevalent in Piedmont and Lombardy. Anti-rabies injections must be given every year and a vaccination log is provided. Apart from rabies and traffic, dogs have fallen victim to porcupines and, terminally, to poisonous snakes. If you live near woods, be careful about letting dogs roam about. One couple in Umbria suspect that their dog was poisoned by their neighbours, who were Sardinian shepherds, because it bothered the sheep. Others have had pets shot, either deliberately or by accident, by the many hunters who scour the woods in Umbria and Tuscany. While discussing hunters, it is important to note that there is no law of trespass in Italy and hunters can hunt over your (agricultural) land. There are rules about discharging rifles, shotguns and airguns a certain amount of metres from occupied houses. To stop hunters tramping over your land - and it is sensible not to be too privacy minded here - a fence two metres high must surround your land. The fence, in one comune, even had to come down the drive, so that hunters and others would not inadvertently come through the gate and then wander over the fields. It must then be clearly stated *Divieto di caccia* (hunting is forbidden).

A few riders have brought their horses to Italy, which is no bad thing because most Italian horses are expensive or not up to much. A Scottish woman at Montecastelli, in Umbria, runs a business buying up Italian horses, getting some condition back on them and selling them on. Horse drugs are expensive in Italy and so is tack, which is far inferior to British or German. Most of the better riding horses come from abroad, although the Maremmano, a draught horse from the Maremma in south west Tuscany, lightened with Thoroughbred, produces a good 15-16.2 hand hunter. Expect to pay £3-4,000. The lady above finds them unpredictable, and prefers to bring on the light-boned 14-15 hand Sardo, Sardinian horse (£1,500). Other saddle horses are the light draught Avigliese, once used for arable farming on hillsides, and Argentinos, which come from Argentina but are now bred in Italy.

In Tuscany and Umbria there is much beautiful wildlife. Little ornamental ponds seem to attract the wild boar for an early morning bathe. They are also prone to dig up shrubs in the garden, as are porcupine. Of the hazards, poisonous snakes are probably the most serious and a bottle of serum should be kept in the fridge and replaced every year. The same serum is used for pets and humans. Snakes are a nuisance as they fall into swimming pools and are quite difficult to kill. Sometimes driving over them does not kill them.

ABOUT THE HOME

There are various ways in which the usual utilities can be connected to your home. If you are buying a flat in a city it is likely that gas, electricity and water will be supplied from the mains. In rural Italy, other arrangements may need to be made and it is best to seek the advice of a *geometra* or knowledgeable neighbour before initiating costly works. The inconvenience of mains supplies not being connected to a house should be reflected in its purchase price.

Gas

The main fuel in Italy is gas. Very few people have oil-fired heating systems and there is no widespread use of fossil fuels (Italy has no indigenous coal). Many people in the country do like wood-burning stoves, and charcoal braziers - the older ones being highly ornamented - are also used (they produce no smoke). But virtually everyone uses gas to cook and heat their water. Those who live in cities and large towns, particularly in the North, are likely to have mains gas provided by *Società Italiana per il Gas*. As with your electricity and telephone, gas bills are lower if you are a resident, that is possessing a *certificato di residenza*. The aim here is to make those owning two homes pay a little more for the privilege. Foreigners who own homes in Italy, and nowhere else, but do not reside there, will pay the higher rate.

In much of rural Italy there is no mains supply of gas. Those wanting central heating, and even Umbria and Tuscany can be cold in winter, will need to obtain a gas storage tank, which usually holds 1,000 litres, and set aside some land, away from the road and the house, where it can be sited. The tank has to be surrounded by a metal fence and have a gate which must be kept locked. The tank cannot be put underground and can, therefore, affect the picturesque appearance of your home. The tank can be filled as many times as you wish, although it is stipulated that you must buy a minimum amount of gas every year (approximately £500). The expense involved in obtaining fuel in this way is only justified if it is required for central heating.

If your home is in a region where the winters are mild, your fuel for cooking will be a *bombola*, a gas bottle. These can be obtained quite easily. They are an expensive and frequently annoying way of cooking. The gas often runs out when you are using the oven for a dinner party and carrying a *bombola* up four flights of stairs because the lift is out of order is an exercise many people would not choose to repeat. However, using *bombole* is often a good deal cheaper than paying to have your flat connected to mains gas, where this is an option, particularly if you do not live there permanently. The price for connection is the same whether you are a resident or not.

If you buy a previously connected house there is no reconnection charge payable by the new owner, provided the current or supply has not been cut off.

Water

Anyone contemplating living in central Italy should read John Mortimer's *Summer's Lease* to get an impression of the problems which can occur with the water supply. Italy suffers from a water shortage. Frequently in summer the supply is cut off altogether during the day, particularly in country areas and in southern towns. Even in flats, it is important to make sure that a storage tank is fitted, so that you can still cook and wash while the supply is off.

Water is supplied by the local comune. There are various types of contract, which differ according to needs. There are special contracts if water is needed for gardens. The general shortage means that obtaining permission for swimming pools is extremely difficult, and in some areas impossible. In the past, many managed to get around these restrictions with the *vasca* scam. A *vasca* is a water basin, which many country people built so that when the comune cut the supply they were not left without any water. In time, however, the authorities began to realise that a disproportionate number of *vasche* were lined with sky blue cement and had what looked suspiciously like a diving board at the end. As a result, there has been a clamp down. However, many of these water tanks are still not connected to the mains. They fill up throughout the winter or are served by nearby springs. It may require some ingenuity, but these *vasche* could perhaps be turned into swimming pools without upsetting anyone. Another problem, of course, is getting permission. Much can depend on the local amenities available, and who owns them.

In more remote areas of the country, where there are no wells, water may have to be delivered in a tanker. This is expensive and inconvenient. Arrangements will have to be made to keep the *vasca* uncontaminated, and the water company will advise on this. Being on the mains supply, whatever its shortcomings, is obviously more convenient. If you buy a house which is not connected to the system, and you want it to be, you will have to pay for this. If pipes need to be laid over neighbours' land, they have to agree. If they won't agree you will have to pay more for the pipes to make a detour. Often pipes are laid on top of the land, which means they can easily freeze in winter.

Electricity

Electricity is supplied by the *Ente Nazionale per l'Energia Electrica*, commonly known as *ENEL*. Bills are usually paid with banker's orders. *ENEL* monitors the amount of electricity you use over two months and then evens things up to estimate your requirements. Bills are paid twice a year.

ENEL is very particular about connecting the supply to new or refurbished houses which have not hitherto been linked to the system. Meticulous checks are made to ensure that the correct type of wires have been used and that all the earthing has been done correctly. It is important to ensure that your electrician is aware of these regulations and is following them - otherwise you will have to generate your own supply, which many people living in remote areas do. This is an arrangement which suits those who want to retreat from the twentieth century. It often means a rather weak current, with no washing machines, dish washers - or TV. The diesel required to run the generators is costly and most people would prefer to be on the mains supply.

Telephone

Getting a telephone installed is one of the major obstacles anyone moving to Italy will encounter. Weeks, months and, for the particularly uninsistent, years can pass without a line being connected. To speed matters along, strings must be pulled summoning up even the most tentative acquaintances. The occasional bribe can be an immense help, although knowing who to bribe can be difficult. In Rome it is reputed that anyone

seriously contemplating a telephone should have £50 put aside
for the purpose. There are additional problems if you live in
remote areas. One family were asked to pay for ten telegraph
poles which would be required to connect them to the phone
system. As each pole was estimated at £50, they are for the
moment continuing to use the public phone in the village bar.
For some reason there is a shortage of lines in many cities and
party lines, with all their irritations, are commonplace.

The public utility which presides over this state of affairs is
the *Società Italiana per l'Esercizio delle Telecomunicazioni*, known as
the *Sip*. Its workings are sufficient to make anyone think that for
all its faults British Telecom has redeeming features. Apart from
the delays in actually getting a telephone line there are several
other grave shortcomings in the service, which is a state
monopoly. Most of the gadgets which have improved the
British telephone service in recent years are officially not
permitted. Thus answerphones should be the approved type
supplied by the *Sip* and cordless phones are not allowed. Of
course, once you have a line it is easy enough to add on any
appliance you like with a little rewiring. But do not be surprised
if on one of his infrequent visits the *Sip* engineer shakes his
head gravely and says such practices are *"vietato"* (forbidden).
More serious for anyone involved in business is the inefficiency
of the service. It is very frustrating to have lengthy faxes, or
modemed information, from abroad interrupted in mid-flow
because the line has been lost. The final insult is that the bills
are seldom very accurate and appeals for a recount are seldom
successful. Bills are usually paid by banker's order.

Bibliography

Doing Business in Italy, prepared by Alegi & Associates, International Legal Consultants, Via XX Settembre 1, 00187 Roma. Or CCH Editions Ltd., Telford Road, Bicester, Oxfordshire OX6 OXD. Tel: Bicester (0869) 253300.
This is an invaluable little booklet which explains in some detail the tax system, employment law, business incentives, arbitration and legal system.

Italy - A Travellers Handbook
Free from the Italian tourist office, this little booklet is full of information: villa rental, golf course, useful addresses, regulations. Contact: Italian State Tourist Office, 1 Princes Street, W1R 8AY. Tel: (01) 408 1254. Or 47 Merrion Square, Dublin 2, Eire. Tel: 766-397/766-025.

Blue Guides to Northern Italy, Alta Macadam; *Southern Italy*, Paul Blanchard; *Sicily*, Alta Macadam.
These are simply the best general guides available. They are authoritative on the main places of interest and have excellent introductions. Sardinia is not covered, however.

Agnelli and the Network of Italian Power, Alan Friedman, Harrap.
Written by the ex-*Financial Times* correspondent in Milan, it questions the role of Italy's de facto royal family, the Agnellis of Fiat. Friedman asks where power lies in *sorpasso* Italy. Not in Rome, it seems.

God's Banker, Rupert Cornwell. Unwin.
An unresolved mystery, no new facts have emerged since the book was written in 1984. A dissection of Italian politics, business and intrigue. Cornwell was the *Financial Times* correspondent in Rome.

The Leopard, Giuseppe di Lampedusa.
One of the best novels since the war, it is essential reading for anyone visiting Sicily. It is set in the time of the Italian Unification, and goes some way to explaining the lack of enthusiasm for it.

Summer's Lease, John Mortimer, Viking.
Molly is a frumpy mum who likes detective stories. She has three children, a solicitor husband and a ghastly old Fleet Street hack for a father. She rents a villa in Tuscany. And there's a mystery. Recently made into a TV series.

The Story of San Michele, Axel Munthe, John Murray.
This charming, sad, self-indulgent book is the autobiography of a man whose life's aim was to live on Capri. Munthe was a fashionable Swedish doctor who practised in Paris, and Rome, at the end of the nineteenth century. His villa at Anacapri, filled with ancient statuary, can be visited.

The Bourbons of Naples, Harold Acton.
An excellent, beautifully written history of the South before Unification. It has not been equalled.

Appendices

Italian government institutions in London where information may be obtained:

Italian Embassy (Chancery), 14 Three Kings Yard, London W1.
Tel: (01) 629 8200

Italian Consulate-General, 38 Eaton Place, London SW1.
Tel: (01) 235 9371

Other consulates

6 Melville Crescent, Edinburgh. Tel: (041) 226 3631
St James's Building, 79 Oxford Street, Manchester. Tel: (061)
236 9024
Vice-Consulate, 7/9 Greyfriars, Bedford. Tel: (0234) 56647

The Italian Chamber of Commerce for Great Britain, 296 Regent
Street, London W1. Tel: (01) 637 3153

Italian Cultural Institute, 39 Belgrave Square, London SW1. Tel:
(01) 235 1461

Italian State Tourist Office, 1 Princes Street, London W1. Tel:
(01) 408 1254

British government institutions in Italy:

British Embassy, Via XX Settembre 80a, 00187 Roma.
Tel: (06) 475 54 41/ 475 55 51.

Consulates

British Vice-Consulate, Via S. Lucifero 87, 09100 Cagliari.
Tel: (070) 65 78 25
British Consulate, Palazzo Castelbarco, Lungarno Corsini 2,
50123 Firenze. Tel: (055) 21 25 94
British Consulate, Via XII Ottobre 2, 16121 Genova.
Tel: (010) 56 48 33/6
British Consulate-General, Via S. Paolo 7, 20121 Milano.
Tel: (02) 80 34 42/ 86 24 90/ 86 24 92
British Consulate-General, Via Francesco Crispi 122, 80122
Napoli. Tel: (081) 66 33 20/ 66 35 11
Rome: same as embassy.
Honorary Consul, Major N.J. Lister, Vicolo delle Ville 16,
34100 Trieste. Tel: (040) 76 47 52
British Consulate, Corso M. D'Azeglio 60, 10126 Torino.
Tel: (011) 68 78 32/ 68 39 21
British Consulate, Accademia 1051, 30100 Venezia.
Tel: (041) 27 207

British estate agents who specialise in selling property in Italy:

Anglo Italian Tourist Centre
Contact: R. Betteley
11 Edgbaston Shopping Centre,
Edgbaston,
Birmingham B16 8SH.
Tel: (021) 4521188
Fax: (021) 4521077

A combined travel and estate agency which has a number of properties in the Lucca area, Tuscany.

Babet
Contact: John Esplen
Tithebarn Babet,
14 High Street,
Godalming,
Surrey GU7 1DL.
Tel: (048 68) 28525
Fax: (048 68) 20661

Has property in three areas: · around San Gimignano (with Volterra and Chianti); north-western Tuscany, around Fivizzano and Aulla; and in Umbria, near Città di Castello.

Barbers
427-429 North End Road,
London SW6 1NX.
Tel: (01) 381 0112
Fax: (01) 385 9144

Property in Chianti, around Cortona, on the Tuscany/Umbria borders, and the Mugello and Val di Sieve, north of Florence.

Brian A. French and Associates,
Contact: Steve Emmet
Suite 3,
12 High Street,
Knaresborough,
North Yorkshire HG5 0EQ.
Tel: (0423) 867047/ 865892
Fax: (0423) 863755

Has a wider network of Italian representatives than any other British-based estate agent. Property is available around Lake Trasimeno, Assisi, Città di Castello (all in Umbria), the Upper Tiber Valley (Umbria/ Tuscany), Arezzo, Montepulciano,

Italian office:
Contact: Marilena Cimadoro
Via S. Chiari 1,
06081 Assisi.
Tel: (075) 816741

Cortona, San Gimignano,
Volterra and Lucca (Tuscany),
Le Marche, Liguria and
Emilia Romagna.

Etruscan Properties
Contact: Ben Foster
The Power House,
Alpha Place,
Flood Street,
London SW3 5SZ.
Tel: (01) 351 5383/ 7556

Specialises in the Lucca area
and has another agent in
Perugia, Umbria.

Exus Italian Homes
Contact: Penny Moses
53 Queen Drive,
London N4 2SZ.
Tel: (01) 800 9093

Has property in Le Marche,
with much around Sarnano,
province of Macerata.

Hamptons
Contact: Phillipa Green
6 Arlington Street,
St James's;
London SW1A 1RB.
Tel: (01) 493 8222
Fax: (01) 493 4921

Hamptons has a number of
large villas for sale
throughout Italy. In Tuscany,
particularly around Lucca, it
offers more modest houses
and flats.

Heart of Tuscany
Contact: Mrs C.M. Cannell
11 Church Street,
Ampthill,
Bedfordshire MK45 2PL.
Tel: (0525) 841404
Fax: (0525) 841404

Company specialises in two
areas in Tuscany: between
San Miniato and Volterra,
which includes the spa town
of Casciana Terme and the
market town of Pontedera.;
and the north-west around
Castelnuovo di Garfagnana
and Barga, in the Apuan Alps.

International Estate Agents,
38 Queens Road,
Brighton,
Sussex BN1 3XB.
Tel: (0273) 24378/ 24419.

Has a range of widely priced
properties in disparate areas
of Tuscany and Umbria. Also
some in Lazio.

Italian Country Homes
Contact: Nikki Keep
Kelly House,
Warwick Road,
Tunbridge Wells,
Kent TN1 1YL.
Tel: (0892) 515611
Fax: (0892) 515883

Houses on offer in Tuscany
around Montespertoli, 20km
south-west of Florence, and in
Chianti. Also properties
throughout Umbria.

Italian Properties
Contact: John Tunstill
Old Telephone Exchange,
Eckington,
Worcestershire WR10 3AP.
Tel: (0386) 750133
Fax: (0386) 750133

Concentrates on the Upper
Tiber Valley around Città di
Castello. Many properties
owned and developed by the
company.

Italian Office
Contact: Fabio Lelli
TAI,
Piazza dell'Incontro 2,
Città di Castello,
(PG) 06012.
Tel: (075) 85 54 208

Property 1992
Contact: James Barnard
74 Elms Crescent,
London SW4 8QX.
Tel: (01) 622 3975
Fax: (01) 978 2383

The company's agents are
based south-east of Siena and
have a selection of property in
Le Crete area. It also has a
limited number of properties
throughout Tuscany and in
Umbria.

Jim & Jill Powrie
Contact: Roger Weaver,
St Helier,
Forest Road,
Brookside,
Ascot,
Berkshire Sl5 8QG.
Tel: (0344) 885005

The Powries have property
for sale along the Upper Tiber
valley: Gubbio, Umbertide,
Città di Castello, Perugia and
into Tuscany around
Sansepolcro.

Italian office
Contact: Jim and Jill Powrie,
Lo Molino,
Via della Barca 136,
06010 Montecastelli,
Umbertide (PG)
Tel: (075) 938179

Rainbow International
Contact: A. Amodio
Kingston House,
7 London Road,
Old Stratford,
MK19 6AE.
Tel: (0908) 567707

Properties in northern
Tuscany around Lucca,
Pistoia and Florence. It also
has seaside flats in Calabria
and around Pescara, in
Abruzzo.

Toscana Limited
Contact: Paola Gibbs
79 Stanhthorpe Road,
London SW16 2EA.
Tel: (01) 769 4586

A range of properties mainly
in the province of Pistoia,
Tuscany.

Tuscany Estates
Contact: Shelley Edgson
Bridge House,
296 Wandsworth Bridge
Road,
London SW6 2UA.
Tel: (01) 736 2891

Company specialises in
property around Lucca.

A list of International Schools in Italy provided by The European Council of International Schools, 21b Lavant Street, Petersfield, Hants GU32 3EL. Tel: (0730) 68244.

Name and address	School head	Age range	Nos. Girls Boys	Fees	Curri- culum
FLORENCE American International School of Florence, Via del Carota 23/25, 50012 Bagno a Ripoli, Firenze. Tel: 055 640033	Roger Frost	3-18	75 65	L4.7m to L7.9m	US
GENOA American International School in Genoa, Via Quarto 13/C, 16148 Genova.Tel: 010 386528	Michael Popinchalk	3-14	45 40	L3.5m to L7m	US
IMPERIA Liceo Internazionale, Piazza Rossini 29, 18100 Imperia. Tel: 0183 20248	John Herbert	13-19	45 45	L4m	UK
MILAN American School of Milan, 20090 Noverasco di Opera, Milano.Tel: 02 5241546	Alan Derry	3-18	190 270	L6.8m to L10.3m	US
International School of Milan, Via Bezzola 6, 20153 Milano.Tel: 02 4524748	Terence Haywood	3-19	270 300	L5.5m to L9m	UK
Sir James Henderson British School of Milan,Viale Lombardia 66, 20131 Milano. Tel: 02 2613299	C. Gill Leech	3-18	200 200	L5.1m to L9m	UK
NAPLES International School of Naples, Mostra d'Oltremare, 80125 Napoli. Tel: 081 635753	Josephine Sessa	3-18	35 35	L5.1m to L9m	UK
ROME Ambrit School, Via Annia Regilla 60, 00178 Roma. Tel: 06 7992907	Bernard Mullane	3-13	90 60	L4.5m to L6m	US/ UK

Name and address	School head	Age range	Nos. Girls Boys	Fees	Curri- culum
American Overseas School of Rome, Via Cassia 811, 00189 Roma. Tel: 06 3664841	Robert Silvetz	3-18	220 210	L4.5m to L12.9m	US
Castelli International School, 13 Via Degli Scozzesi, 00046 Grottaferrata.Tel: 06 9459977	Marianne Palladino	5-14	0 30	L5.9m	US/ UK
Greenwood Garden School, Via Vito Sinisi 5, 00189 Roma. Tel: 06 3666703	Donna Siebert Ricci	2.5-6	18 17	L2.5m to L4.8m	US .
International Academy of Rome, Via di Grottarossa 295, 00189 Roma. Tel: 06 3666071	Joanna Bulgarini	3-10	50 40	L4.4m to L6.6m	US/ UK
Kendale Primary International School, Via Gradoli 83, Tombe di Nerone, 00189 Roma. Tel: 06 3667608	Veronica Tani	3-10	50 40	L4.4m to L6.6m	US/ UK
Marymount International School, Via di Villa Lauchli 180, 00191 Roma. Tel: 06 3290671	Anne Marie Hill	4-19	260 50	L4.9m to L11.5m	US
New School, Via della Camilluccia 669, 00135 Roma.Tel: 06 3284269	Josette Fusco	3-18	45 45	L4m to L10.9m	UK
Notre Dame International School, Via Aurelia 796, 00165 Roma. Tel: 06 6808801	Joseph Umile	10-18	30 170	L10.5m	US
Rome International School, Via Morgagni 25, 00161 Roma. Tel: 06 856994	Gillian Bennet	3-12	20 20	L5.m to L7.8m	UK
Southlands English School, Casal Palocco, Via Epaminonda 3, 00124 Roma. Tel: 06 6090932	Vivien Frances- chini	3-13+	70 70	L4.2m to L7.2m	UK

Name and address	School head	Age range	Nos. Girls Boys	Fees	Curri- culum
St George's English School, Via Cassia KM 16, 00123 Roma. Tel: 06 3790141/2/3/	Colin Niven	3-18	440 410	L6.8m to L11.5m	UK
St Stephen's School, Via Aventina 3, 00153 Roma. Tel: 06 5750605	Gary Crippen	13-19	86 74	L10.9m	US
Summerfield School SRL, Via Tito Poggi 21, Divino Amore 00134 Roma. Tel: 06 7955227	Ann Morgia	3-8	14 24	L2m to L6.6m	UK
TRIESTE International School of Trieste, Via Conconello 16, Opicina, 34100 Trieste. Tel: 040 211452	Peter Metzger	2-16	72 88	L3.2m to L6.5m	US
United World College of the Adriatic, Via Trieste 29, 34013 Duino (TS). Tel: 040 208822	D.B. Sutcliffe		100 100		
TURIN American Cultural Association of Turin, Vicolo Tiziano 10, 10024 Moncalieri. Tel: 011 645967	Richard Gillogly	3-18	100 65	L5.5m to L9.2m	US
VARESE European School, Via Montello 118, 21100 Varese. Tel: 0332 285062	Willi Krueger	4-18	590 585	BF 3,500 to BF 14,000	
VENICE The International School, The British Centre, San Marco 4267a, Venezia. Tel: 041 5286612	John Millerchip	5-11	20 20	L5.4m	UK

British-based consultants in Italian law (supplied by The Law Society, 50 Chancery Lane, London WC2A 1SX. Tel: 01 242 1222)

Griffinhoofe
6 Stone Buildings, Lincoln's Inn,
London WC2A 3XT.
Tel: (01) 404 0786

Specialises in residential property. George Pazzi-Axworthy is a solicitor also qualified in Italian law.

Dr Giuseppe Cala
The Cloisters, Temple, London
EC4Y 7A.
Tel: (01) 353 5424

Carnelutti and Carnelutti
Quality Court, Chancery Lane,
London WC2A 1HP.
Tel: (01) 242 2268

Studio Legale Bisconti
Gillet House, 55 Basinghall Street,
London EC2V 5DU.
Tel: (01) 606 0416

Mainly deals with commercial and corporate law.

Nello Pasquini
Middleton Potts, 3 Cloth Street,
Long Lane, London EC1A 7LD.
Tel: (01) 600 2333

Baker and McKenzie
Aldwych House, Aldwych,
London WC2B 4JP.
Tel: (01) 242 6531

Mainly commercial. Offices in Milan and Rome.

Amhurst Brown Collombotti
2 Duke Street, St James's,
London SW1Y 6BJ.
Tel: (01) 930 2366

P.L. Elliott
2nd Floor, 44 Bedford Row,
London WC1R 4LL.
Tel: (01) 831 9396

Associates in Rome.

Payne Hicks Beach
10 New Square, Lincoln's Inn,
London WC2A 3QG.
Tel: (01) 242 6041

Office in Rome.

Penningtons
37 Sun Street, London EC2M 2PY.
Tel: (01) 377 2855

Claudio Del Giudice, of
Penningtons, writes frequently on
issues affecting Italian property
law.

Pritchard Englefield and Tobin
23 Great Castle Street, London
W1N 8NQ.
Tel: (01) 629 8883

Offices in Milan and Rome.

Italian lawyers in Italy who correspond in English and provide details to the Law Society. Other languages (where available) are indicated after the lawyer's name.

AGRIGENTO

Dr Vicenzo Campo, Via Bac Bac 45, 92100 Agrigento.

ALBENGA

Avv Santino Durante (French/ German), Via Medaglie d'Oro 48, 17031 Albenga.

ANCONA

Avv Giacomo Vettori, Via Calatafimi 2, Ancona.

AREZZO

Avv Antonio Niccolai, Via Madonna del Prato 96, Arezzo.

AVELLINO

Avv Arturo Iaione, Via Trinità 55, 83100 Avellino.

BARI

Prof Avv Aldo Regina, Via Melo 185, 70121 Bari.
Avv Bruno Amendolito, Viale Lenin 23, 70122 Bari.
Avv Raffaele Barile, Via Cairoli 57, 70122 Bari.
Avv Pier Luigi Casasarano, Via Marchese di Montrone 106, 70122 Bari.
Dott Proc. Angelo Stella, Via Principe Amedeo 320, 70122 Bari.

BOLOGNA

Avv Paola Caldini, Via Albergati 19, Bologna.
Avv Prof G Bernini, Via Mascarella 94/96, Bologna.

BORDIGHERA

Avv G. Moreno, Via V. Emanuele 131, 18012 Bordighera.

BRESCIA

Avv Angelo Carattoni (French), Corso Magenta 43/d, Brescia. Tel: 0365 43777.

BRINDISI

Avv Pompeo Vergine, Corso Umberto 72, 72100 Brindisi.

CALTANISSETTA

Avv Rosario Asaro, Corso V. Emanuele 109, 93100 Caltanissetta.

CATANIA

Avv Alessandro Attanasio (French), Via Ramondetta 31, 95128 Catania.
Avv Adele Fischetti, Via Vecchia Ognina 19, 95131 Catania.
Avv Vincenza Palermo, Via Vecchia Ognina 19, 95131 Catania.
Avv Angela Chimento, Via Francesco Riso 42, 95128 Catania.

CATANZARO

Avv Aldo Ferrara, Via Buccarelli 27, 88100 Catanzaro.
Avv Giuseppe Sirianni, Via Francesco Crispi 125, 88100 Catanzaro.

CHIAVARI

Avv F. Bacigalupo (French), Corso Gianelli 11, 16043 Chiavari.

COSENZA

Avv Angelo Mario Manes, Via Mygi, 87038 San Lucido, Cosenza.

FLORENCE

Enrico Ciantelli (German/ French. Legal adviser to German consulate), Via dei Servi 9, 1-50122 Firenze. Tel: 055 215352.
Studio Contri and Puccini (Legal advisers to British, US and Swiss consulates), Via G. Pico della Mirandola 9, 50132 Firenze. Tel: 055 579259.
Avv Fulvio Faraoni, Viale S. Lavagnini 41, Firenze.

FOGGIA

Avv Antonio Lioia, Via San Angelo 3, 71100 Foggia.

GENOA

Avv Alberto Castagnoli (French. Legal adviser to British Chamber of Commerce, Italy. Member of New York Bar Association), Corso Andrea Podestà 11-8, 1-16128 Genova. Tel: 010 590700.
Avv Vernarecci & Associati (French/ German), Via Garibaldi 3, 1-16124 Genova. Tel: 010 205876
Avv Massimo Medina (French. Legal adviser to British Consulate), Via S. Sebastiano 15, Genova.

GROSSETO

Avv G. Padovani, Via Garibaldi 44, Grosseto.

JESOLO

Avv Antonio Forza, Piazza Drago, 30017 Lido di Jesolo.
Avv P. Serrentino, Via Mameli 36, 30017 Lido di Jesolo.

LECCE

Avv Marino Lazzari, Via Cosimo de Georgi 7, 73100 Lecce.
Avv Alfredo Lonoce, Viale Brindisi 11, 73100 Lecce.
Avv Giacomo Lisi, Via Salvatore Grande 3-b, 73100 Lecce.
Avv Michele Tarantino, Viale dello Stadio 53, 73100 Lecce.
Proc. Roberto Scariglia, Via dei Perroni 10, 73100 Lecce.

LIVORNO

Dott Vittorio Carelli, Via dei Carabinieri 28, Livorno.

LUCCA

Avv Alberto del Carlo, Piazzale Ricasoli 241, Lucca.

MACERATA

Avv Canzio Strinati, Corso Cavour 50, Macerata.

MATERA

Avv Ottavio Lonigro, Via Rocca Scotellaro 11, 75100 Matera.

MESSINA

Avv Antonio Gemelli (French/ German), Via Pippo Romeo n4, 1-98123 Messina. Tel: 090 780156

Avv Carlo Vermiglio (French), Via Nino Bixio 89, 1-98123 Messina. Tel: 090 2938581

Avv.ti Martino-Fiertler-Palumbo (French/ German), Via Maddalena 42, 1-98100 Messina.

Avv Giorgio Mirti della Valle, Via P. Romeo 4, 98100 Messina.

Avv Giuseppe Toscano, Via Maffei 13, 98100 Messina.

MILAN

Avv Bruno & Associati (French), V P. Verri 10, 1-20121 Milano. Tel: 02 706996/ 798823.

Avv Alberto Cajola (Legal adviser to British Chamber of Commerce), Via G. Rossini 5, 1-20122 Milano. Tel: 02 709305/ 796720

Avv Alberto Castagnoli (French), Studio Danovi, Via Guastalla 15, 1-20122 Milano. Tel: 02 798351.

De Berti & Jacchia (French. De Berti, barrister, member of Gray's Inn), Foro Buonaparte 20, 1-20121 Milano. Tel: 02 809486.

Studio Legale Gilioli (French. Partners members of American Bar), Piazzale Principessa Clotilde 8, 1-20121 Milano. Tel: 02 6559732.

Scamoni e Associati (French/ German/ Dutch/ Spanish), 11-A Piazza della Repubblica, 1-20124 Milano. Tel: 02 6596501.

Avv Ughi & Nunziante (French), Via Sant'Andrea 19, 1-20121 Milano. Tel: 02 793951.

D.B. MacFarlane (Legal adviser to British Consulate), Via Visconti di Modrone 32, 1-20122 Milano.

Avv Luzzatto (French/ German), Via Visconte Modrone 12, 1-20122 Milano.

Avv Guido Frati (French), Via Daniele Crespi 2, 1-20123 Milano.

Avv Ruggero di Palma Castiglione (French/ German), Via Ciovasso 11, 1-20121 Milano.

MONTECATINI TERME

Avv Giovanni Marchetti, Via dei Colombi 2, Montecatini Terme.

NAPLES

Comito Viola & Partners (French/ German/ Spanish), Viale Gramsci 17/B, 80122 Napoli. Tel: 081 680634/ 663086.

Avv Manlio Cicatelli (French), Parco Margherita 85, 80121 Napoli.

Avv Lucio Conte, Viale Elena 19, 80122 Napoli.
Prof Avv Paolo Tesauro, Via Toledo 156, 80134 Napoli.
Avv Bruno Castaldo, Via A. Depretis 14, 80133 Napoli.
Avv Giuseppe Fonisto, Via Diaz 15, 80055 Portici (NA).
Avv Giuseppe Iannelli, Calata San Marco 4, 80133 Napoli.

PADUA

Avv Giuseppe Majolino, Riviera Ponti Romani 6, 35121 Padova.
Avv Vittorio Vangelisti, Studio Gasparini, Via Altinate 47, 35121 Padova.

PALERMO

Avv Mario Solina, Via Le Farina 13-A, 90141 Palermo.
Avv Ivo Ferrara, Studio Legale Acampora, Via Torricelli 32, 90145 Palermo.

PERUGIA

Studio Legale Scassellati Sforzolini (French), Piazza Piccinino 13, 06100 Perugia. Tel: 075 25244/5.

PESARO

Dott Proc Marco Paolini, Via S. Francesco 30, Pesaro.

PIETRASANTA

Avv F. Luchi, Via XX Settembre 25, (Versilia) Pietrasanta.

PISA

Avv Proc Enrico Cortese, Piazza Donati 5, Pisa.
Avv Renato Tortorella, Piazza del Pozzetto 3, Pisa.

PISTOIA

Avv Pietro Lacava, Via della Repubblica 12, Pistoia.

PORDENONE

Avv Pompeo Pitter, Piazza XX Settembre 21, 33170 Pordenone.
Avv Sebastiano Scata, Via Bertossi 13, 33170 Pordenone.

POTENZA

Avv Aldo Morlino, Via N. Sole 73, 85100 Potenza.

PRATO

Enrico Ciantelli (French/ German. Legal adviser to German consulate), Via Valentini 8-D, 50047 Prato. Tel: 40940.
Avv Girgio Pratesi (French), PO Box 556, 50047 Prato. Tel: 0574 24665.

RAVENNA

Avv Carlo Lobetti, Via Boccaccio 6, Ravenna.
Avv Emilio de Mari, Via D'Azeglio 1, Ravenna.
Avv Massimo Stranghellini-Perilli, Via XIII Giugno 4, Ravenna.

RIMINI
Avv Eugenio della Valle, Piazza Cavour 8, Rimini.
ROME
Avv Piero Amenta (French), Piazza Augusto Imperatore 4, 00186 Roma. Tel: 06 6879033/ 6796488.
Studio Legale Paolo Arangio-Ruiz (French), Via Marziale 36, 00136 Roma. Tel: 06 310640/ 310650.
G. Egidio International Law Office (French), Via Archimede 59, 00197 Roma. Tel: 06 3603807/ 3603746
John Greaves, Via Adige 20, 00198 Roma. Tel: 06 8458143/ 8440812.
Avv Raimondo Marini-Clarelli (French), Tel: 06 864049/ 868508. All correspondence to: Payne, Hicks Beach & Co, 10 New Square, Lincoln's Inn, London WC2A 3QG. Tel: 01 242 6041.
Avv Ferruccio Mengaroni (French, German), Via della Camilluccia 35, 00135 Roma. Tel: 344117.
Ughi & Nunziate (French), Via XX Settembre 1, 00187 Roma. Tel: 06 476841.

SALERNO
Avv Michele Alfano, Via Canale 8, 84104 Nocera Inferiore (SA)
Avv Edilberto Ricciardi, Via Amendola 36, 84100 Salerno.
SALO
Avv Angelo Carattoni (French), Piazza Fossa Cond. Gasparo, 25087 Salo. Tel: 0365 43777
SAN REMO
Avv Osvaldo Moreno (French), Via Roma 176, 18038 San Remo.
Avv F. Moreno (French), Via N. Bixio 21, 18038 San Remo.
SAVONA
Studio Calamaro & Rosso (French), Piazza Rovere 3-6, 17100 Savona.
SIENA
Avv Fausto Arrighi, Via di Città 25, Siena.
SYRACUSE
Avv Massimo Cannizzo, Via Adda 33, 96100 Siracusa.
Dott Proc Giuseppe Saetta, Via Adda 33, 96100 Siracusa.
LA SPEZIA
Avv F.A. Borachia (French/ German), Via Ratazzi 29, 19100 La Spezia.
Avv E. Forcieri, Via Cavour 3, 19100 La Spezia.
Avv.ti E. & D. Toracca (German/ Spanish), Piazza Battisti 21, 19100 La Spezia.

TARANTO

Avv Armando Lasaivia, Piazza Giovanni XXIII 20, 74100 Taranto.
Avv Mario De Francesco, Via F. De Palma 82, 74100 Taranto.

TURIN

Studio Avv Calonna (French), Corso Siccardi 11, 1-10122 Torino. Tel: 011 511423/ 550272.

TRAPANI

Avv Michele Lombardo, Via Vespri 2, 91100 Trapani.
Avv Vito Lombardo Bonanno, Via Vespri 83, 91100 Trapani.
Avv Domenico Vivona Molinari, Via Blundo 11, 91013, Trapani.

TREVISO

Avv Piero Gritti, Via Canoniche 12, 31100 Treviso.
Dr Proc Carlo Mosca, Via Dall'Oro 39, 31100 Treviso.

UDINE

Avv Gianni Giunchi, Vicolo Porta 5, 33100 Udine.

VENICE

Enzo Morelli (French/ German), Campo SS Filippo e Giacomo 4512, 1-30122 Venezia.Tel: 041 5223228/ 5236558
Avv Alberto Malacart, (Adviser to British Consul) S Sofia, Cannaregio 4001/B, 30125 Venezia.
Avv Ferruccio Solveni (French), Dorsoduro 376-B, 30123 Venezia.

VENTIMIGLIA

Avv E. Laura (French), Corso della Repubblica 20, 18039 Ventimiglia.

VERONA

Avv Silvio Marzari e Colleghi (German), Via Amatore Sciesa 10, 1-37122 Verona. Tel: 045 8343/ 8006878.

VICENZA

Avv Giancarlo Castegnaro, Contrada Canove 17, 36100 Vicenza.

Accountants associated with the Institute of Chartered Accountants, Gloucester House, 399 Silbury Boulevard, Central Milton Keynes MK9 2HL. Tel: (0908) 668833.
(• indicates an overseas organisation associated with a member firm - no partner/director is a member of the Institute)

ANCONA

Price Waterhouse, Via Corridoni 2, 60100 Ancona.

BARI

Coopers & Lybrand, Piazza Umberto 49, 70121 Bari.
Grant Thornton International, Via Sparano 115, 70121 Bari.

BERGAMO

• Serca Snc, Via Divisione Julia 7, 24100 Bergamo.

BOLOGNA

Arthur Andersen & Co, Piazza Malpighi 4/2, 40123 Bologna.
Arthur Young & Co, Via della Zecca 2, 40121 Bologna.
Deloitte Haskins & Sells, Via Gallena 21, 40121 Bologna.
Grant Thornton International, Via Parigi 13, 40121 Bologna.
Price Waterhouse, Via dell'Indipendenza 2, 40121 Bologna.
Reconta Touche Ross (A.C. Kavanagh), Via Saragozza 1, 1-40123 Bologna.
Thomas (TRM) & Co, (T.R.M. Thomas), Via F. Baracca 10, Casalecchia di Reno, 40033 Bologna.
Touche Ross International, Via Saragozza 1, 1-40123 Bologna.

FLORENCE

Deloitte Haskins & Sells, Via Cavour 64, 50129 Firenze.
Ernst & Whinney, Via Delle Belledonne 16, 1-50123 Firenze.
Reconta Touche Ross, Via La Pira 17, 1-50100 Firenze.
Touche Ross International, Via La Pira 17, 1-50100 Firenze.

GENOA

Arthur Andersen & Co, Piazza Della Vittoria 15, 16121 Genova.
Deloitte Haskins & Sells, Via XX Settembre 10, 16121 Genova.
Moore Stephens, 1 Piazza Corvetto, 16122 Genova.
Price Waterhouse, Via Fieschi 3/14, 16121Genova.

MESSINA

Moore Stephens, Corso Cavour 31, Isolato 291, 98100 Messina.

MILAN

Arthur Andersen & Co, Via della Moscova 3, 20121 Milano.
Arthur Young & Co, (J.A. Stewart), Via Conservatorio 15, 20122 Milano.

• **Binder Dijker Otte & Co**, Piazza del Liberty 4, 20121 Milano.
Coopers and Lybrand SAS, Via Vittor Pisani 20, 20124 Milano.
Deloitte Haskins & Sells, Via Monte di Pietà 24, 20121 Milano.
Ernst & Whinney, (M.A. Pimm) Via Cornaggia 10, 1-20123 Milano.
Fidirevisa Italia (M.E. Golding), Via Senato 12, 20121 Milano.
Grant Thornton International, Via Durini 18, 20122 Milano.
Hodgson Landau Brands, Corso Porta Romana 13, 20122 Milano.
Humphreys & Gates (J.F. Gates) Piazza Velasca 5, 20122 Milano.
• **KPMG Fides Certificazione**, Via Vittor Pisani 22, 20124 Milano.
Moore Stephens, Via Cosimo del Fante 16, 20122 Milano.
• **Moret & Limperg**, Via Conservatorio 15, 20122 Milano.
Peat Marwick Mitchell, (D.J.B. Herrera) Piazza F. Meda 3, 20121 Milano.
Price Waterhouse (L.C. Khanna, J.C. Kothari), Corso Europa 2, 20122 Milano.
Price Waterhouse, Via della Signora 2/N, 21022 Milano.
Reconta Touche Ross (D.W.P. Lawton), Corso Garibaldi 49, 1-20121 Milano.
• **Serca SNC**, Via S. Senato 2, 20122 Milano.
Spicer & Oppenheim, Via Paolo da Cannobio 11, 20122 Milano.
Studio Aletti (M.F. Neale) Via Amadei 15, 20123 Milano.
Touche Ross International, Corso Garibaldi 49, 1-20121 Milano.

MODENA

Ernst & Whinney, 1 Portici, Viale Buon Pastore, 248-1-41100 Modena.
Reconta Touche Ross, Via Carlo Sigonio 50, 1-41100 Modena.

NAPLES

Arthur Young & Co, Via Filangieri 21, 80121 Napoli.
Coopers & Lybrand, Viale Gramsci 17/B, 80122 Napoli.
Ernst & Whinney, Via Carlo Poerio 15, 1-80121 Napoli.
Hodgson Landau Brands, Via Emanuele Gianturco 50/A, 80146 Napoli.
Price Waterhouse, Via del Rione Sirignano 7, 80121 Napoli.

PADUA

Arthur Young & Co, Piazza Salvemini 13, 35100 Padova.
Coopers & Lybrand, Largo Europa 16, 35100 Padova.
Price Waterhouse (A. von Gebsattel), Via Carlo Cassan 34, 35100 Padova.

PALERMO

• **KPMG Fides Certificazione**, Via Marchese Ugo 52, 90141 Palermo.
Reconta Touche Ross, Via Alfonso Borelli 3, 1-90139 Palermo.
Touche Ross International, Via Alfonso Borelli 3, 1-90139 Palermo.

PISA
• **KPMG Fides Certificazione,** Via Toselli 17, 56100 Pisa.
PARMA
Price Waterhouse, Viale Tanara 20/A, 43100 Parma.
ROME
Arthur Andersen & Co, Via Compania 47, 00187 Roma.
Arthur Young & Co, Via del Pozzeto 105, 00187 Roma.
Coopers & Lybrand, (R. Ware, T.S. Choo), Via delle Quattro Fontane 15, 00184 Roma.
Deloitte Haskins & Sells, (L.E. Milen), Via Flaminia 495 (Ponte Milvio), 00191 Roma.
Ernst & Whinney, Via Abruzzi 25, 1-00187 Roma.
Grant Thornton International, Via Donizetti 7, 00185 Roma.
Hodgson Landau Brands, Viale Regina Margherita 192, 00198 Roma.
• **KPMG Fides Certificazione,** Via Sicilia 66, 00187 Roma.
Mathison (John), (J. Mathison), Via Zandonai 75, 00194 Roma.
Moore Stephens, Via Archimede 164, 00197 Roma.
Peat Marwick Mitchell, Via Sardegna 40, 00187 Roma.
Price Waterhouse, Via Aniene 30, 00198 Roma.
Reconta Touche Ross, Via del Governo Vecchio 3, 1-00186.
Sturgess (David), (D.A. Sturgess), Studio di Consulenza Aziendale, Via Vinicio Cortese 180, 00128 Roma.
Touche Ross International, Via del Governo Vecchio 3, 1-00186 Roma.
TREVISO
Arthur Andersen & Co, Piazza San Vito 37, 31100 Treviso.
Clark (Martin) (G.M. Clark), Via 14 Maggio 1944, 1/A 31100 Treviso.
TURIN
Arthur Andersen & Co, Galleria San Federico 54, 10121 Torino.
Arthur Young & Co, Via Giolitti 5, 10123 Torino.
Coopers & Lybrand SAS, Corso Vittorio Emanuele 97, 10128 Torino.
Deloitte Haskins & Sells, Corso San Maurizio 79, 10124 Torino.
•**Dunwoody Robson MaGladrey & Pullen,** Via Giovanni Prati 2, 10121 Torino.
Ernst & Whinney, Via Amendola 12, 1-10121 Torino.
Hodgson Landau Brands, Corso Re Umberto 12, 10121 Torino.
•**KPMG Fides Certificazione,** Corso Vittorio Emanuele 11, 10128 Torino.
Price Waterhouse, Conte G. Bogino 23, 10123 Torino.
Price Waterhouse, Via Rona 255, 10123 Torino.
Reconta Touche Ross, Via Cavour 1, 1-10123 Torino.
Spicer & Oppenheim, Via XX Settembre 3, 10121 Torino.
Touche Ross International, Via Cavour 1,1-10123 Torino.

VENICE

Hodgson Landau Brands, Via Verdi 33, Mestre 30172 Venezia.
Reconta Touche Ross, Via Filippo Grimani 1, Mestre 1-30174 Venezia.
Touche Ross International, Via Filippo Grimani 1, Mestre 1-30174 Venezia.

VERONA

Coopers & Lybrand SAS, Via Malenza 2, 37121 Verona.
Ernst & Whinney, Via A. Mario 10, 1-37121 Verona.
• **KPMG Fides Certificazione**, Corso Cavour 39, 37121 Verona.
Spicer & Oppenheim, Corso Porta Nuova 99, 37122 Verona.

VICENZA

Deloitte Haskins & Sells, Contra San Faustino 12, 36100 Vicenza.
Humphreys & Gates, Via Garpagnon 11, 36100 Vicenza.

PLACES OF WORSHIP

Catholic churches for English-speaking people:

ROME   San Silvestro, Piazza San Silvestro.
                         S. Tomaso di Canterbury, Via di Monserrato 45.

Irish Catholic churches:

ROME   Sant'Agata dei Goti, Via Mazzarino.
                         San Clemente, Via San Giovanni in Laterano.
                         St Patrick's, Via Boncompagni 31.
                         Sant'Isidoro, Via degli Artisti.

Anglican churches :

ALASSIO   St John, Via Cardellino 21, 17021 Alassio.

ASSISI   At the Church of San Gregorio al Mango. Tel: 812 238.

BARI   Served from Naples. Information from Mrs Renzulli, Via Ceglia 5, 70010, Valenzano, Bari. Tel: 87 718 98.

CADENABBIA   Church of the Ascension, summer only. Tel: 40685.

CAPRI   Served from Naples at the Church of Santa Sofia, Anacapri.

FLORENCE   St Mark, Via Maggio 18, 50125 Firenze. Tel: 294 764. The Ven G.L.C. Westwell.

GENOA   Church of the Holy Ghost, Piazza Marsala 3, 16122 Genoa. Tel: 56 48 33. Revd H.W. Sanderson.

LARGO PATRIA Served from Naples. Enquire locally from Nato personnel.

MILAN   All Saints, Via Solferino 17, 20121 Milano. Tel: 655 22 58. Revd G.A.C. Brown.

NAPLES   Christ Church, Via S Pasquala a Chiaia 15b, 80121 Napoli. Tel: 411 842. Revd P.J.W. Blackburn.

PALERMO   Holy Cross, Via Mariano Stabile. Tel: 58 17 87. Revd M. Harper.

ROME	All Saints, Via del Babuino, Piazza di Spagna, 00187 Roma. Tel: 679 43 57. Revd B. Wardrobe.
SAN REMO	All Saints, Corso Matuzia 1, 18038 San Remo.
SIENA	St Peter. Served from Florence April to October. Tel: 972 84.
SORRENTO	At RC Cathedral. Served from Naples. May to July, and September.
TAORMINA	St George, Via Pirandello 10, 98039 Taormina.
TRIESTE	Served from Venice at St Anastasio, Via Manna 6.
VARESE	Served from Milan at Chiesa Evangelica, Via Verdi, 21100 Varese. Tel: 76 60 48.
VENICE	St George, Campo San Vio, 30123 Venezia. Tel: 520 0571. Revd Dr W. Baar.

Episcopal Church of the United States of America:

FLORENCE	St James Church, Via Bernardo Rucellai 13, 50123 Firenze. Tel: 294 417. Revd S.H. Hartman.
ROME	St Paul's Church, Via Napoli 58, 00184 Roma. Tel: 46 33 39. Revd Canon E. Todd.

Scottish Presbyterian:

GENOA	Church of the Holy Ghost, Piazza Marsala.
ROME	St Andrew, Via XX Settembre 7. Tel: 64751672

Methodist churches:

FLORENCE	Via dei Benci 9.
GORIZIA	Via Diaz.
ROME	Piazza Ponte Sant'Angelo.
	Via Firenze 38.

Synagogues:

ALESSANDRIA	Via Milano 15. Tel: 62224.
ANCONA	Via M. Fanti 2. Tel: 202638.
BOLOGNA	Via Gambruti 9.
CASALE MONFERATTO	Vicolo Salomone Olper 44. Tel: 34240
FERRARA	Via Mazzini 95. Tel: 47004.

FLORENCE	Via L.C. Farini 4.
GENOA	Via G Bertora 6. Tel: 891513.
LIVORNO	Piazza Grande, Via del Tempio 3. Tel: 24290.
MANTUA	Via G. Govi 11. Tel: 321490.
MERANO	Via Schiller 14. Tel: 23127.
MILAN	Great Synagogue: Via Guastalla 19. Tel: 731851.
	Ashkenazi Synagogue: Via Cellini 2.
	Beth Shelomo: Corso di Porta Romana 63.
	New Synagogue: Via Eupili 8.
MODENA	Piazza Mazzini 26. Tel: 223978.
NAPLES	Via S.M.A. Capella Vecchia 31. Tel: 416386.
PADUA	Via S. Martino e Solferino 5-7. Tel: 23524.
PARMA	Vicolo Cervi 4.
PISA	Via Palestro 24. Tel: 27269
ROME	Orthodox Italian Service, Lungotevere Cenci. Tel: 6785051.
	Via Balbo 33.
	Orthodox Sephardi Service: Via Catalana.
	Orthodox Ashkenazi Service: Via A. De Pretis 77.
SENIGALLIA	Via dei Commercianti.
SIENA	Via delle Scotte 14.
TRIESTE	Via S. Francesco d'Assisi 19. Tel: 768171.
TURIN	Via San Pio V, 12. Tel: 682387.
URBINO	Via Stretta.
VENICE	There are 5 synagogues. Details from Rabbi A. Piatelli, Cannaregio 1189, Ghetto Vecchio. Tel: 715012.
VERCELLI	Via Fòa 70.
VERONA	Via Rita Rosani.
VIAREGGIO	Via degli Oleandri 30.

GLOSSARY OF USEFUL TERMS

Agente immobiliare - estate agent

Agriturismo - countryside tourism, now deemed an agricultural activity

Ammistratore - administrator, such as in a block of flats

Avvocato - lawyer

Camorra - Neapolitan *mafia*

Caparra - (*caparra confirmatoria*) deposit in part-payment for property.

Carta bollata - legally stamped documents, which add to the general tedium of Italian bureaucracy

Casa rurale - a "rural house", so designated in the local land office. It is, or has been, used as a working farm.

Casa urbana - "urban house", is also a land registry designation, which applies to all property which is not dependent on its surrounding land. A "casa urbana" can be in the middle of the countryside with not a neighbour in sight.

Casa colonica - old type of farmhouse, often with animal stalls on the ground floor

Catasto -land office

Certificato di residenza - residency certificate, very important for tax purposes

Commercialista - general financial adviser

Clientelismo - "clientism", Italian term for old boys' network

Collaudo - an MOT for a car

Coltivatore diretto - a "direct cultivator", who has the first right to buy all rural property which borders his/her property.

Compromesso - preliminary sales contract for the property, more correctly called the *contratto preliminare*

Concessione edilizio - planning permission

Condominio - condominium

Geometra - surveyor

Imposta - tax

Mutuo - a mortgage

'Ndrangheta - Calabrian *mafia*

Notaio - public notary

Permesso di soggiorno - police permission to reside in Italy

Vendesi - "for sale"

Vietato - forbidden

Index

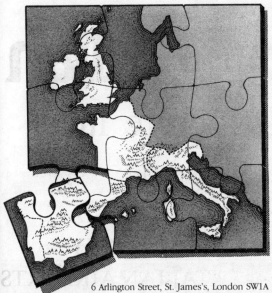